KEVIN McCOLLUM   JEFFREY SELLER   ROY MILLER
LAURA CAMIEN   KRIS STEWART   VINEYARD THEATRE

present

[title of show]

Music and Lyrics by	Book by
JEFF BOWEN	**HUNTER BELL**

Starring

HUNTER BELL   **SUSAN BLACKWELL**   **HEIDI BLICKENSTAFF**   **JEFF BOWEN**

and

COURTNEY BALAN   **BENJAMIN HOWES**

Scenic Design	Costume Design	Lighting Design	Sound Design
NEIL PATEL	**CHASE TYLER**	**KEN BILLINGTON** **JASON KANTROWITZ**	**ACME SOUND** **PARTNERS**

Casting	Technical Supervisor	Production Stage Manager	Vocal Arrangements
TELSEY + COMPANY	**BRIAN LYNCH**	**MARTHA DONALDSON**	**JEFF BOWEN** **LARRY PRESSGROVE**

Associate Producers

RACHEL HELSON   **SARA KATZ**   **LAMS ENTERTAINMENT**   **JAIMIE MAYER**
HEATHER PROVOST   **TOM SMEDES**

Press Representative	Marketing	Promotions	General Management
SAM RUDY **MEDIA RELATIONS**	**SCOTT A. MOORE**	**HHC MARKETING**	**THE CHARLOTTE** **WILCOX COMPANY**

Musical Direction & Arrangements

LARRY PRESSGROVE

Directed and Choreographed by

MICHAEL BERRESSE

Originally presented at the 2004 New York Musical Theatre Festival
[title of show] was partially developed at The Eugene O'Neill Theater Center.
The producers wish to express their appreciation to Theatre Development Fund for its support of this production.

Opening night July 17, 2008

www.titleofshow.com

ISBN 978-1-4234-7382-4

T0056340

WILLIAMSON MUSIC®

A RODGERS AND HAMMERSTEIN COMPANY

www.williamsonmusic.com

EXCLUSIVELY DISTRIBUTED BY

HAL•LEONARD®
CORPORATION

7777 W. BLUEMOUND RD. P.O. BOX 13819 MILWAUKEE, WI 53213

Visit Hal Leonard Online at
www.halleonard.com

[about *title of show*]

[title of show] began its journey on a brown couch in midtown New York City, in April, 2004. Our thirties were underway, and the time had come for us to make the move from outside observers to inside achievers in the business of show. So, we decided to document the process of creating a musical and turn that very process into just that: a musical.

An email from a friend alerted us of the New York Musical Theatre Festival and its submission deadline of May 3rd, a mere three weeks away. We wrote day and night, and about five minutes before the post office closed on the 3rd, we ran there (the inspiration for the logo), postmarked the envelope and sent our baby on its way.

I think we both knew when we walked out on the street after mailing that envelope that day that our lives had changed forever. Next we assembled our intrepid team of collaborators (Larry Pressgrove, Susan Blackwell, Michael Berresse, and Heidi Blickenstaff) and the six of us began to turn this work of autobiofictionography into a living piece of theatre. We made our way through workshops, readings, rehearsals, and retreats, with a side order of sweat, tears, dreams, low lows and high highs. And all of it continued to inspire and shape *[title of show]*.

Our journey included off-off broadway (manhattantheatresource), a festival (NYMF), a summer workshop (The O'Neill Center), another brief New York run (Ars Nova), an extended off-Broadway run (The Vineyard Theatre) and ultimately we arrived four years later on Broadway at the historic Lyceum Theatre.

The often-used phrase "labor of love" is an understatement as it applies to *[tos]*. We love this show. We love the family it created and the fortunes and surprises it continually gives us.

The book you are holding in your awesome, vampire-killing hands that you're too nervous to bend back the spine and break in for fear of the pages coming worn and loose, should indeed be broken in and worn out. Being able to share the mechanics of this music and these lyrics (and select dialogue) is like opening our toy chest for all the neighborhood kids to have a go at our games, trucks and action figures.

So play it, sing it, dance it! Alone...with family...with cast mates or "besties." In a practice room...in your basement...for your recital...for your summer stock pals at three AM...in your choir room on your lunch break...or for the audition of a lifetime... wherever. And when you do play it, sing it, or dance it, we hope you can feel the joy that we had writing it, performing it, and living it—and ultimately our sense of pride, happiness and love for our musical, *[title of show]*.
— *Jeff Bowen and Hunter Bell*

For Michael, Larry, Heidi, Susan, Laura, Kevin, Martha, Tom, Benjamin, Courtney, Stacia, Dale, Harris, Mary, Matt, Jen, Leah, our brothers and sisters-in-law, our moms and dads...and all [tos]sers everywhere on the planet...maybe even outer space.

[about jeff bowen]

JEFF BOWEN (Music and Lyrics) was awarded an OBIE for *[title of show]* as well as the Jim Owles Human Rights Award, and a Broadway.com Audience Award. The show also earned GLAAD Media and Drama League nominations for Best Musical. Jeff has written music and lyrics for the 2007 Easter Bonnet competition for Broadway Cares/Equity Fights AIDS, the Actors Fund 125th Anniversary Gala, the Vineyard Theatre's 25th Anniversary Gala, the 53rd Annual Drama Desk Awards, *Broadway Bares 18: Wonderland*, Sonnet Repertory Theatre, Broadway in South Africa and Walt Disney Imagineering Creative Entertainment. He has composed music for several shows at P.S. 122 including *Avant-Garde-A-Rama in Sparklevision, Hello, My Name Is Avant-Garde-A-Rama, Sparklefest 2000* at Dixon Place; *The A-Train Plays*; and the film *Boat Mime*. Jeff received a BA in theatre and music from Stetson University. He is a member of The Dramatists Guild, ASCAP, The Yale Dramatic Association, The National Audubon Society and The Nature Conservancy.

[about hunter bell]

HUNTER BELL (Book) earned an OBIE Award, a GLAAD Media nomination, a Drama League nomination, and a 2009 Tony® Award nomination for Best Book of a Musical, all for *[title of show]*. Other credits include the book for *Silence! The Musical*, the book for the 137th edition of the Ringling Bros. and Barnum & Bailey circus, *Bellobration!*, and original material for Walt Disney Imagineering Creative Entertainment. He has contributed material to numerous benefits and events including the Easter Bonnet and Gypsy of the Year competitions as well as *Broadway Bares*, all for Broadway Cares/Equity Fights AIDS. He is also a co-creator of the web series "the *[title of show]* show" on titleofshow.com. Born in Tuscaloosa, Alabama, Hunter is a proud graduate of Woodward Academy, a distinguished alumnus of Webster University's Conservatory of Theatre Arts (where he earned a BFA in Musical Theatre), a member of The Dramatists Guild, and a certified card-carrying vampire killer.

[contents]

UNTITLED OPENING NUMBER

Words and Music by
JEFF BOWEN

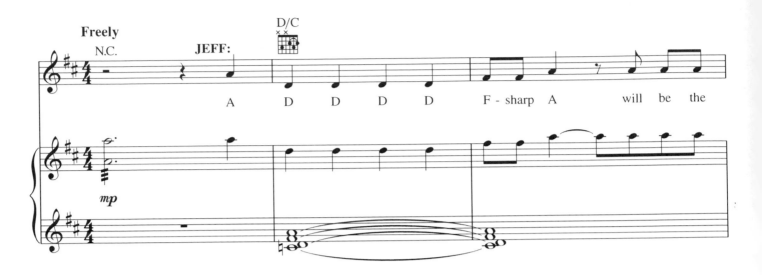

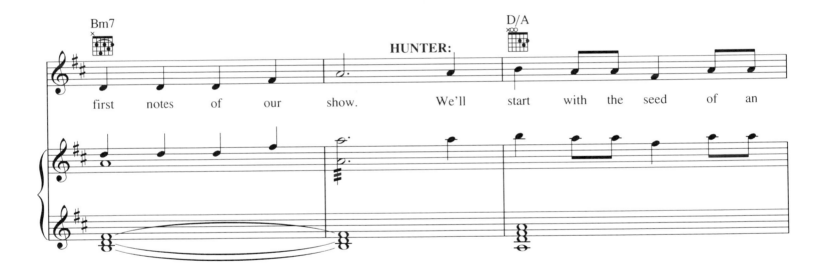

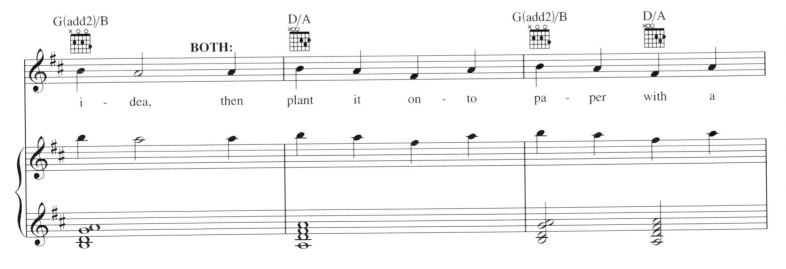

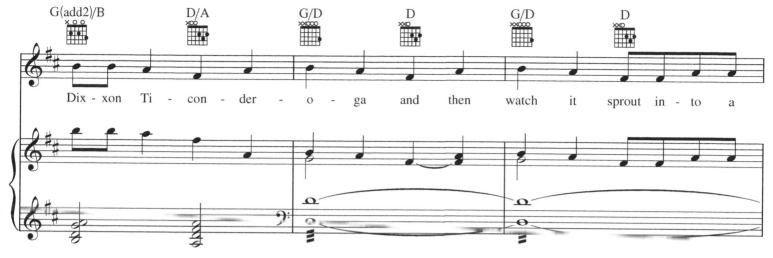

Dix-xon Ti-con-der-o-ga and then watch it sprout in-to a

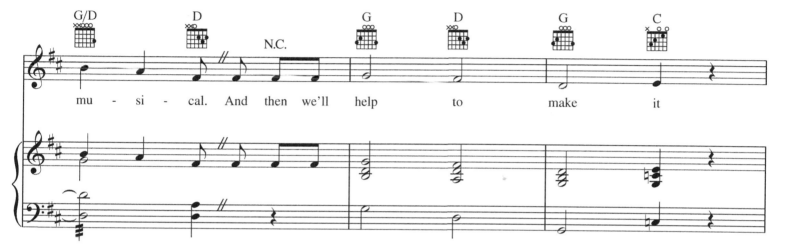

mu-si-cal. And then we'll help to make it

Moderately fast Pop Show Tune

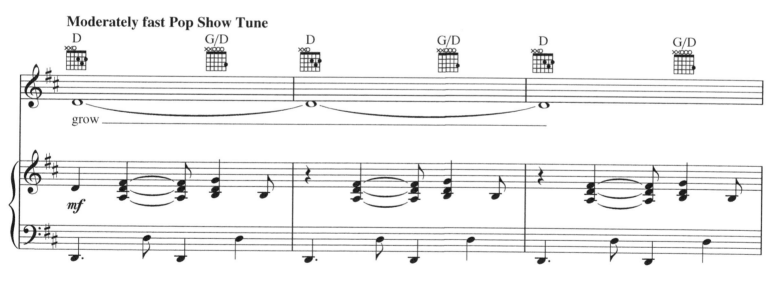

grow

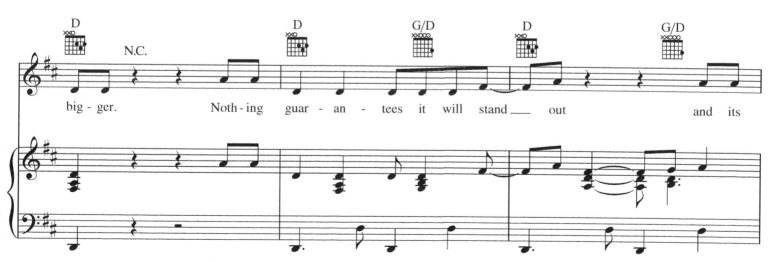

big-ger. Noth-ing guar-an-tees it will stand out and its

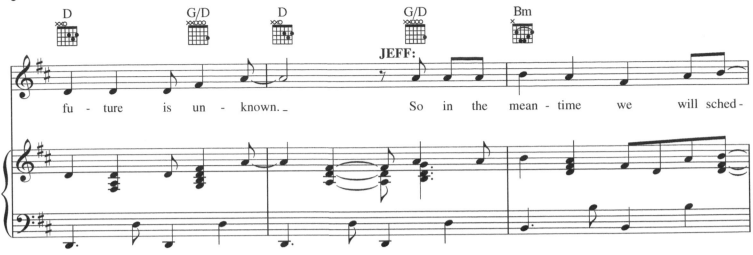

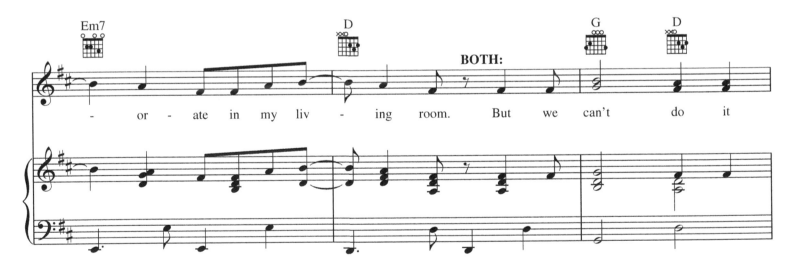

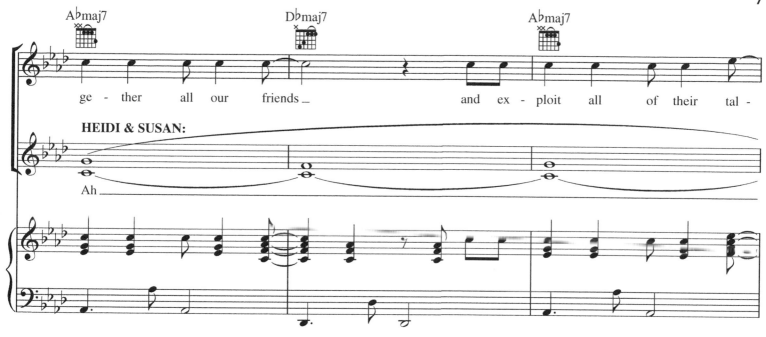

ge - ther all our friends __ and ex - ploit all of their tal -

HEIDI & SUSAN:

Ah __

- ents. We'll ex - plore the lat - est trends __ and a -

Ah __

void them when we bal - ance the book with the score, __

try-ing hard not to du-pli-cate___ what we've seen___ and heard be-fore.___

Ooh_____ ooh_____

___ And if Bar-tok's here he'll ap-pre-ci-ate___ if we're in-

___ ooh_____

ven-tive with the score.___ So we'll put in a syn-co-

ooh.___

ALL (Women 8vb):

10

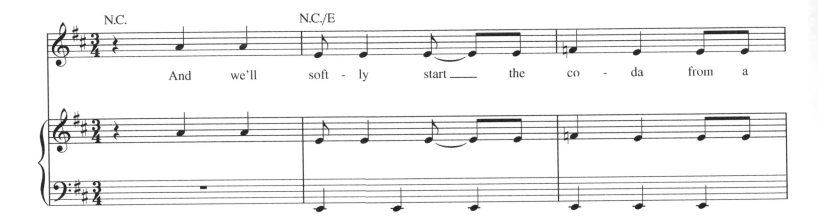

TWO NOBODIES IN NEW YORK

Words and Music by
JEFF BOWEN

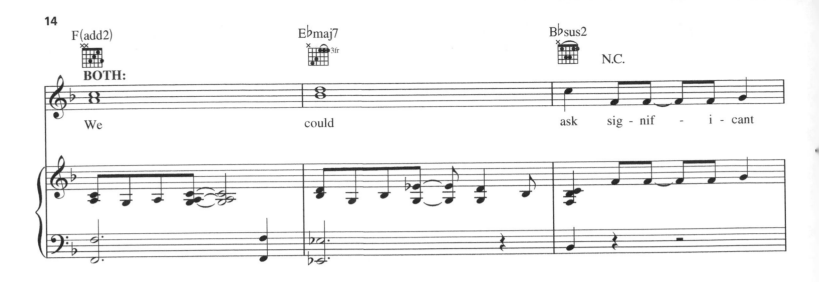

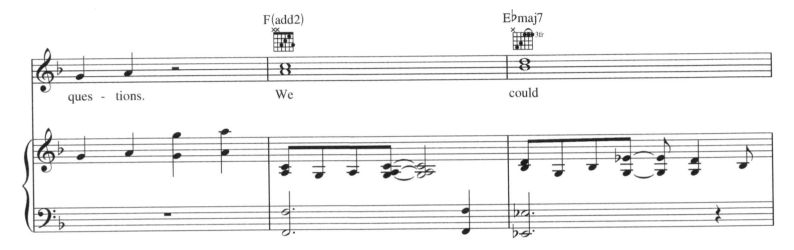

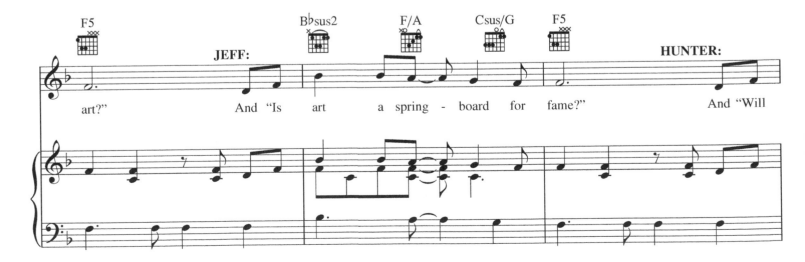

fame get____ folks to trust us?" But will they trust us if it's

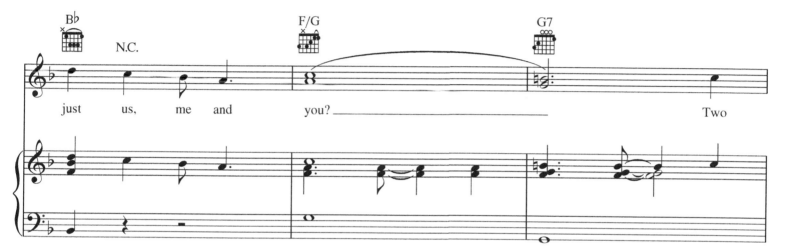

just us, me and you?_____ Two

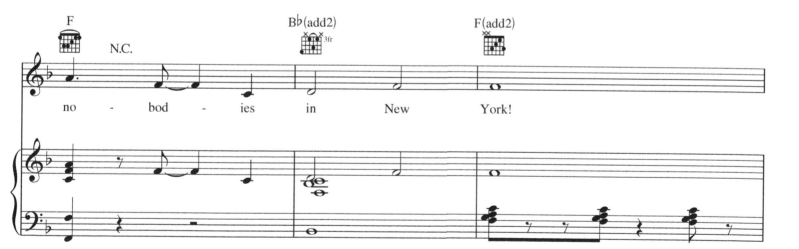

no - bod - ies in New York!

HUNTER:

Hey,____ I think it's work-ing, we're dis - cov-er-ing choic - es, lots____

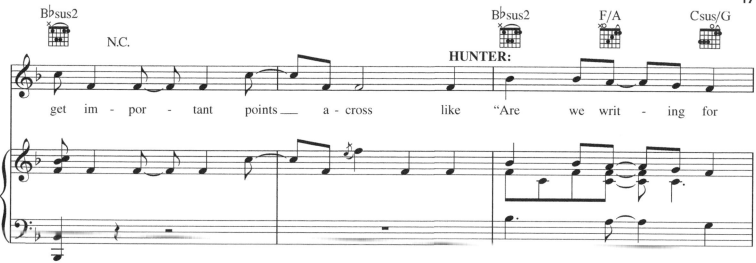

get im - por - tant points ___ a - cross like "Are we writ - ing for

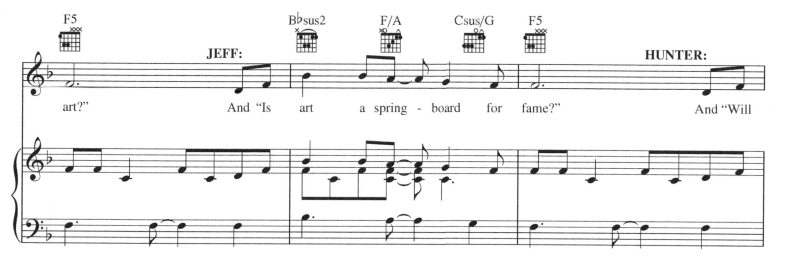

art?" **JEFF:** And "Is art a spring - board for fame?" **HUNTER:** And "Will

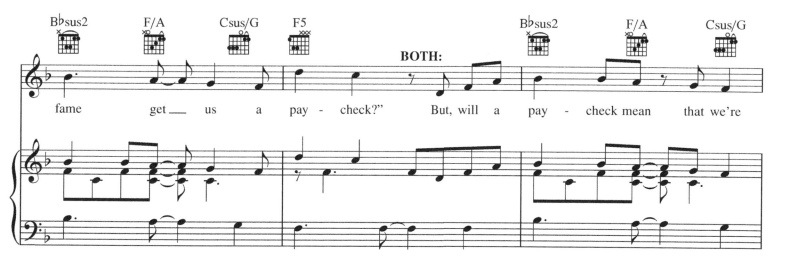

fame get __ us a pay - check?" **BOTH:** But, will a pay - check mean that we're

sell - outs? And if we sell - out, will they yell out me and

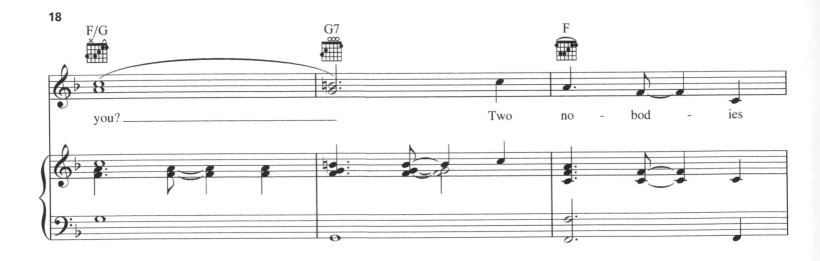

you? _____ Two no - bod - ies

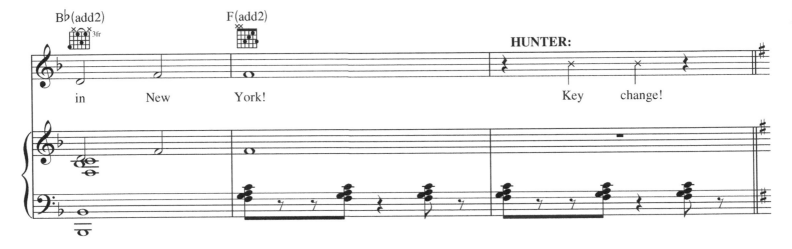

in New York! Key change!

HUNTER:

JEFF:
May - be some day __ our show will get a thea - tre and __ if not this fes - ti - val then

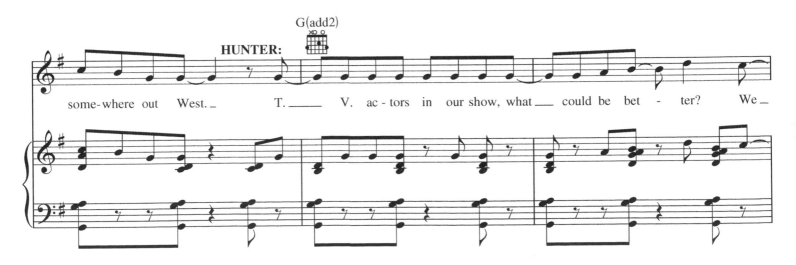

some - where out West. _ T. ___ V. ac - tors in our show, what __ could be bet - ter? We _

HUNTER:

JEFF: *Sweeter!*
HUNTER: *What?*
JEFF: *Sweeter! We've been over this a million times.*
You know the lyric is "sweeter."
HUNTER: *But, here's the deal: One of them sounds like*
it's two syllables and the other sounds like it's three
syllables. So it's "swee-ter"; "the-a-tre." Does that rhyme?
JEFF: *Yes. I'm sorry, Larry. From the key change.*

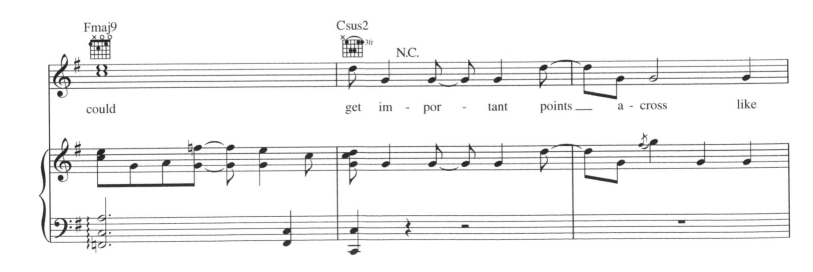

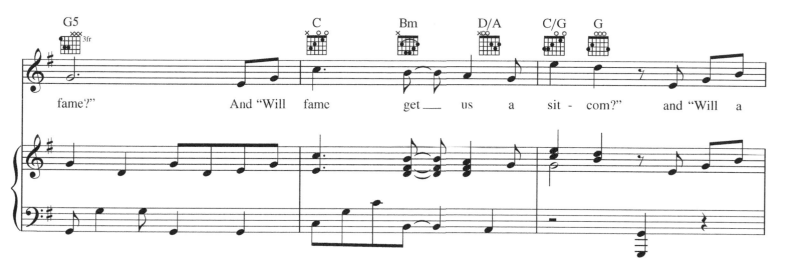

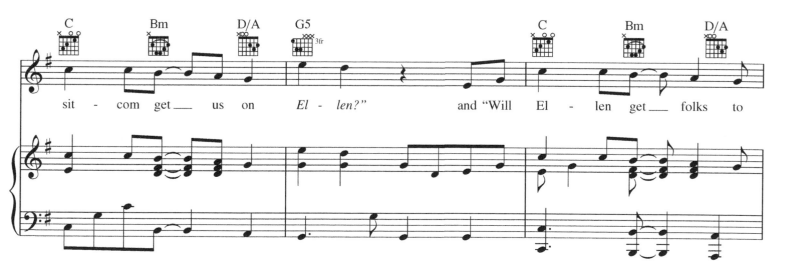

AN ORIGINAL MUSICAL

Words and Music by
JEFF BOWEN

BLANK PAPER*: *Hey little guy, why so blue?*
JEFF: *Well, Blank Paper, I'm trying to write an original musical and I'm a little stuck.*
BLANK PAPER: *Well, cracker, why don't I give you a crash course on how to go from a*
blank piece of paper to a full-tilt boogie Original Musical!
JEFF: *Did you just call me a cracker? Is this character black?*
BLANK PAPER: *Motherfucker, I can be anything you want me to be. That's the point!*

I'm an o - rig - i - nal mu - si - cal, o -

rig - i - nal mu - si - cal. Those oth - er shows can step to the rear. ___ If you

lend me your ear, I'm gon - na ease all your fear and prove that all you need is what's right up here.

* *The role of BLANK PAPER was played by Hunter.*

24

BLANK PAPER: *You see a lot of times musicals are based on books, like* The Scarlet Pimpernel, *and other times they're based on plays like* Spring Awakening. *But more recently, musicals have been based on movies, like* Shrek, The Little Mermaid, Mary Poppins, Hairspray, Billy Elliot, The Lion King, Legally Blonde, 9 to 5, Spamalot…

JEFF: *So movies make good musicals?*

BLANK PAPER: *Well, they make musicals.*

JEFF: *I'm trying to write a musical about two guys writing a musical about two guys writing a musical.*

BLANK PAPER: *That sounds like some crazy shit, bitch! But it's original and I like that. Sing with me!*

JEFF: *Okay, I will!*

25

BLANK PAPER: *Easy, motherfucker! Broadway? Let's start with Off or Off-Off Broadway.*
JEFF: *But why can't I dream big?*
BLANK PAPER: *Well if it was a jukebox musical, a revival or a recognizable commodity,*
I'd say dream away bi-atch. But, original on Broadway? Baby, that ain't
gonna happen unless you've got some stars in mind.
JEFF: *Well, we'd love to have Alice Ripley. She's fierce. Hey, that's the first time I've ever said fierce! That's the second!*
BLANK PAPER: *Playa, I mean TV stars, movie stars, pop stars...like Toni Braxton or Ashlee Simpson.*

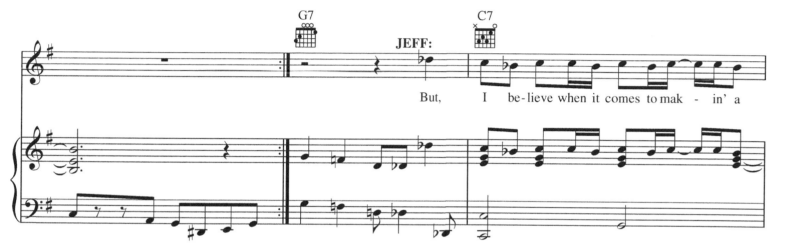

they want a name! ___ An au - di - ence wants to see ___ Par - is

JEFF: *Who wants to see Paris Hilton as Mame?*
BLANK PAPER: *I don't know. A lot of people. Shit! Your ass is crazy, motherfucker, but I like you.*
You may just be crazy enough to fuckin' fuckity fuck succeed motherfucker...
JEFF (Interrupting): *What's with all the foul language? Is that appropriate or even necessary?*
BLANK PAPER: *If you don't like it make me say something else. I am your Blank Paper!*
I'll say whatever you want me to. Just put your pen to the paper and write!
JEFF: *Okay! I will, I will! I'll write!*
BLANK PAPER: *Now we're talking!*

Hil - ton in *Mame!* ___

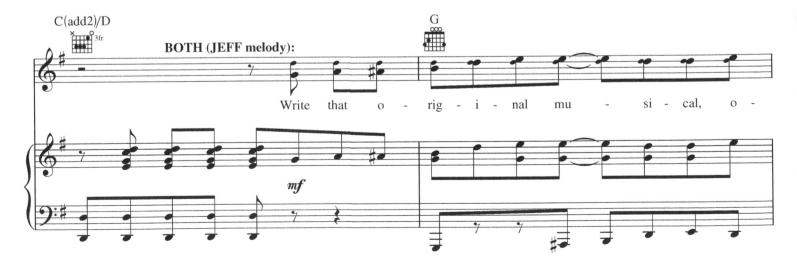

BOTH (JEFF melody):

Write that o - rig - i - nal mu - si - cal, o -

MONKEYS AND PLAYBILLS

Words and Music by
JEFF BOWEN

Bor - row or Steal, Buck White, Big Deal and Bring Back Bird - ie and

Ba - gels and Yox.

Ah. _____

SUSAN: *Close your eyes. Breathe. Ladle into that barrel of monkeys you call a head and scoop out an image monkey.*

_____ There's Hur - ry, Har - ry,

Hap - py as Lar - ry, Mar - i - lyn and Ver - y Warm for May. _____

32

Moderately fast, crisp groove

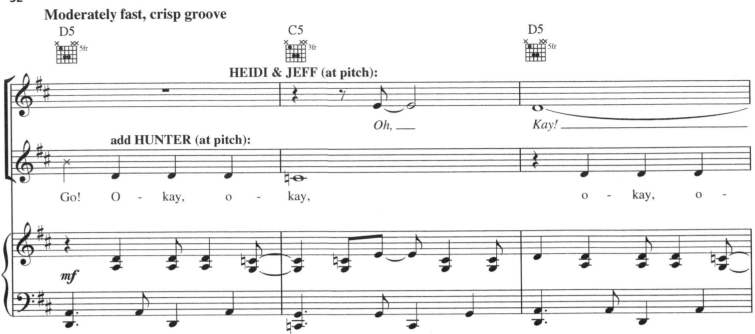

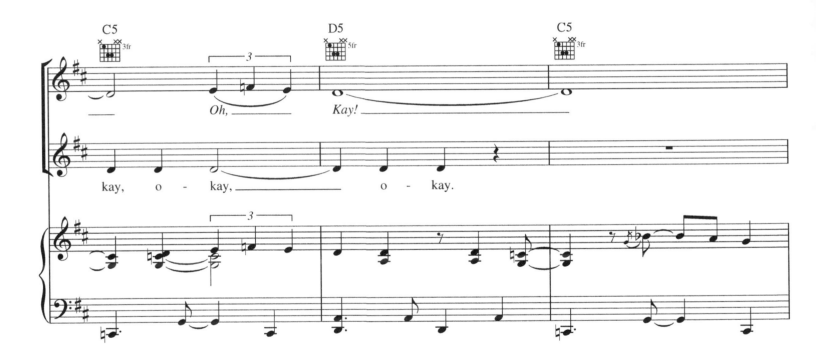

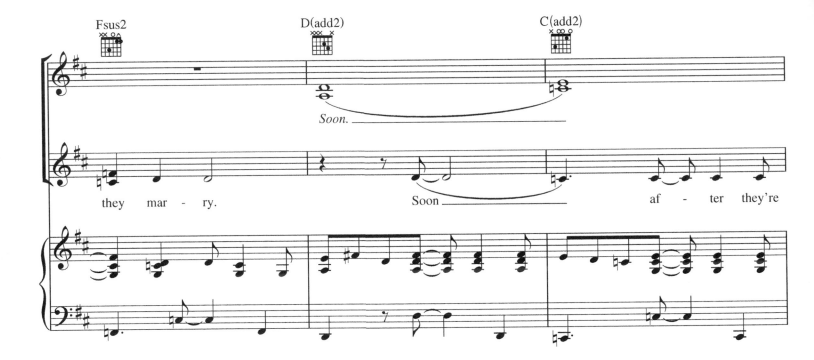

Times. *Wild and* *Won - der - ful.*

times *it _____ was* *wild and* *won - der - ful.*

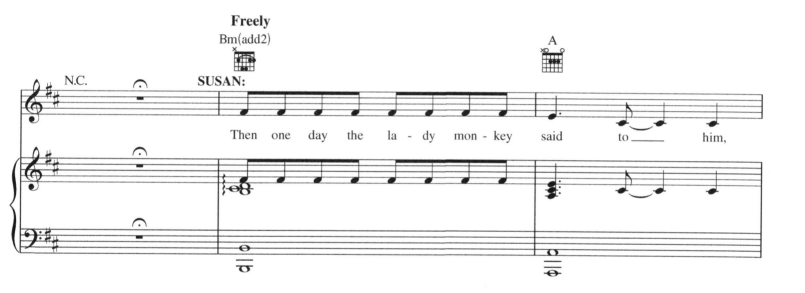

Freely

SUSAN:

Then one day the la - dy mon - key said to _____ him,

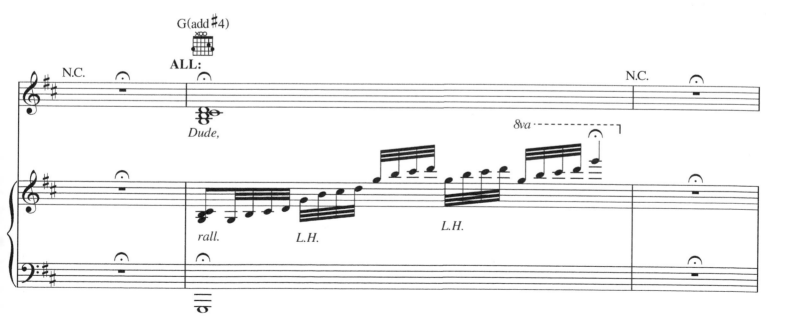

ALL:

Dude,

rall. *L.H.* *L.H.* *8va*

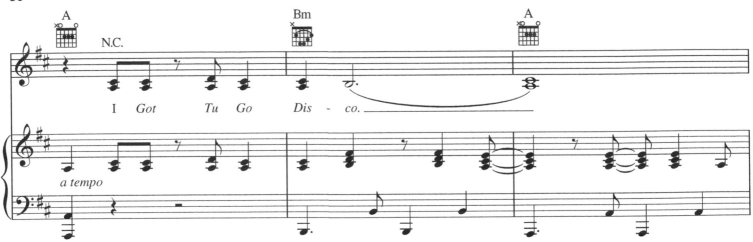

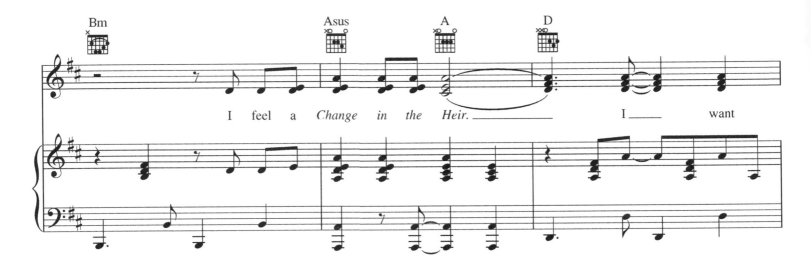

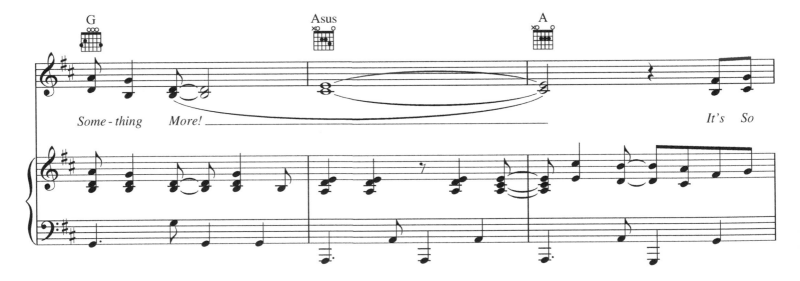

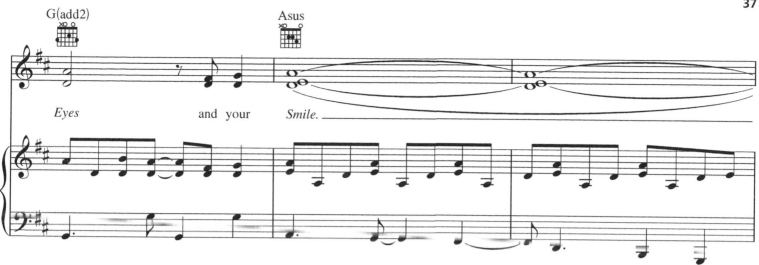

Eyes and your *Smile.*

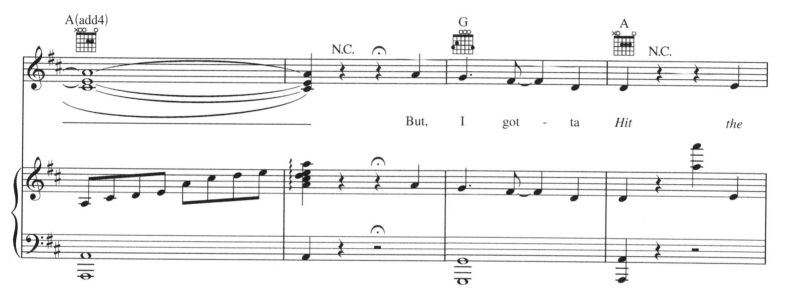

Eyes. But, I got - ta *Hit* the

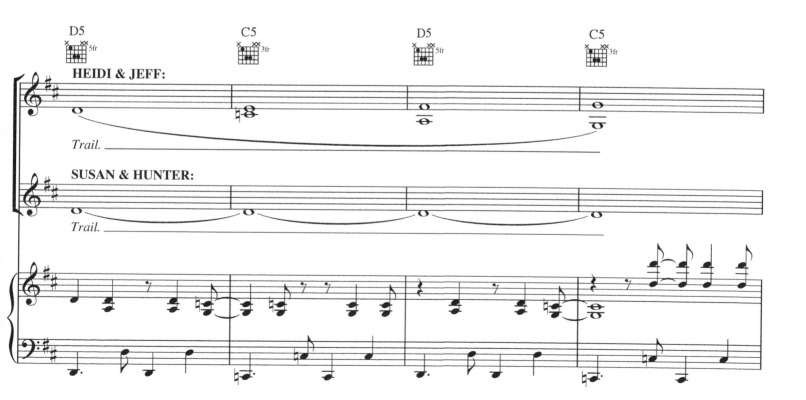

HEIDI & JEFF:

Trail.

SUSAN & HUNTER:

Trail.

Just me and my speed - boat, ___ *Mer - ri - ly We Roll A -*

Just me and my speed - boat, ___ *Mer - ri - ly We Roll A -*

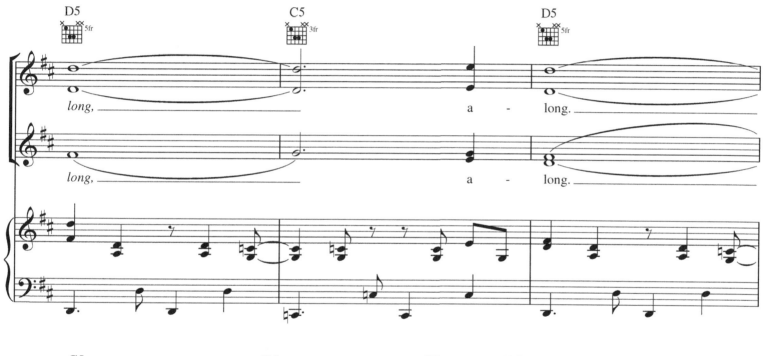

long, _____ *a* - *long.* _____

long, _____ *a* - *long.* _____

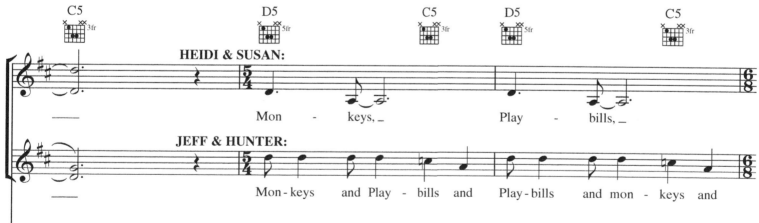

HEIDI & SUSAN:

Mon - keys, ___ Play - bills, ___

JEFF & HUNTER:

Mon - keys and Play - bills and Play - bills and mon - keys and

mon - keys,   mon - keys and   Play - bills,

mon - keys and Play - bills and   mon - keys and   Play - bills and mon - keys and

Play - bills and   mon - keys, _____   Play - bills. _____

Play - bills and   mon - keys, _____   Play - bills. _____

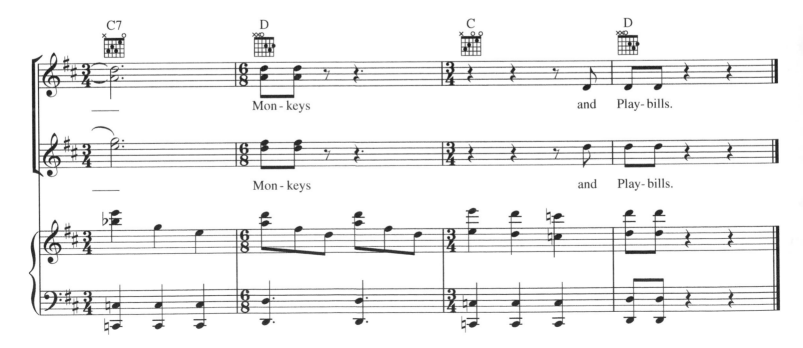

_____ Mon - keys   and   Play - bills.

_____ Mon - keys   and   Play - bills.

PART OF IT ALL

Words and Music by
JEFF BOWEN

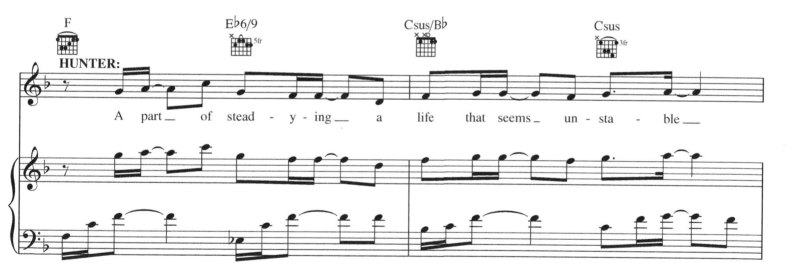

HUNTER:

A part __ of stead - y - ing __ a life that seems __ un - sta - ble __

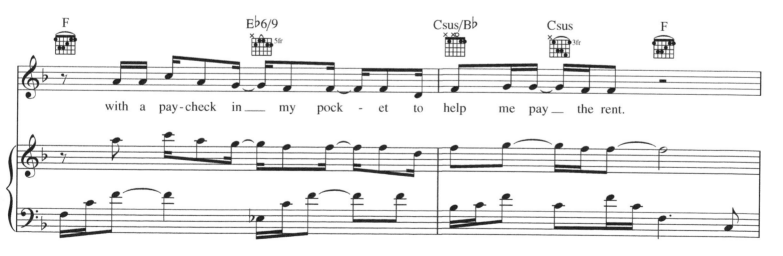

with a pay-check in __ my pock - et to help me pay __ the rent.

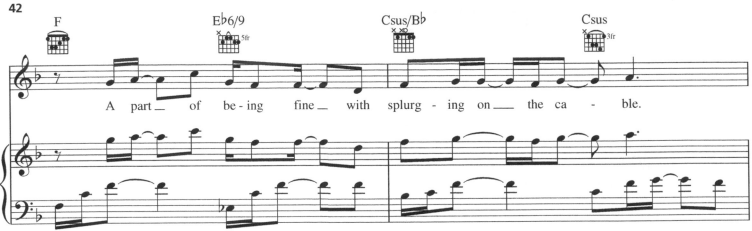

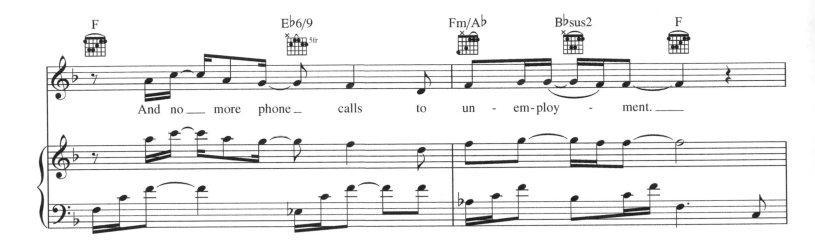

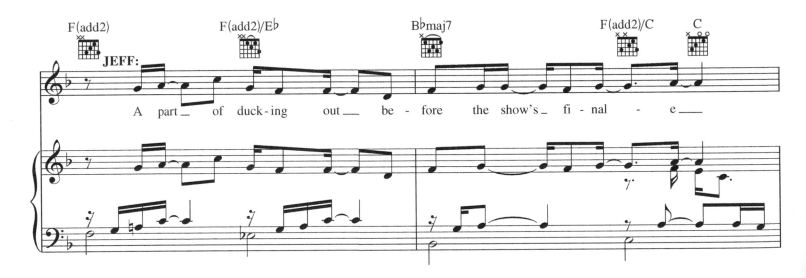

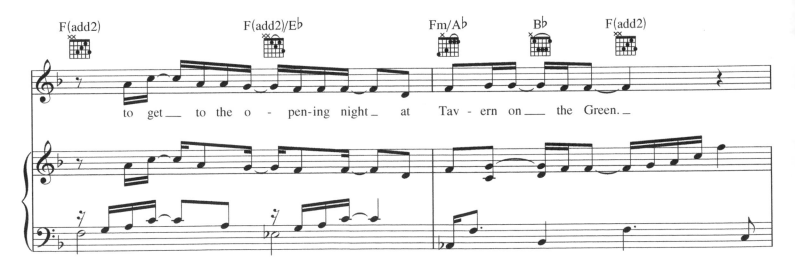

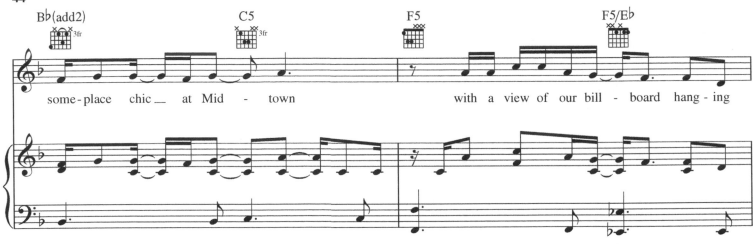

some-place chic __ at Mid - town   with a view of our bill - board hang - ing

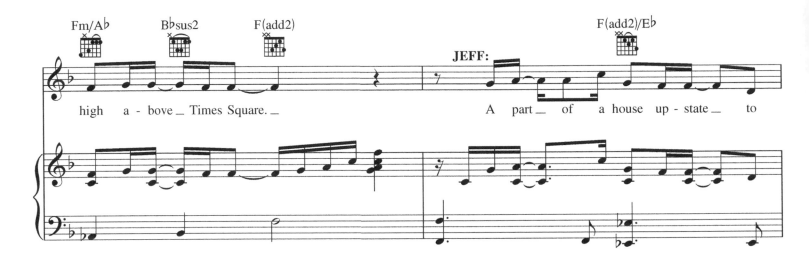

JEFF:

high a - bove __ Times Square. __   A part __ of a house up - state __ to

spend the week wind - ing down   while our mu - si - cals __ are play - ing from

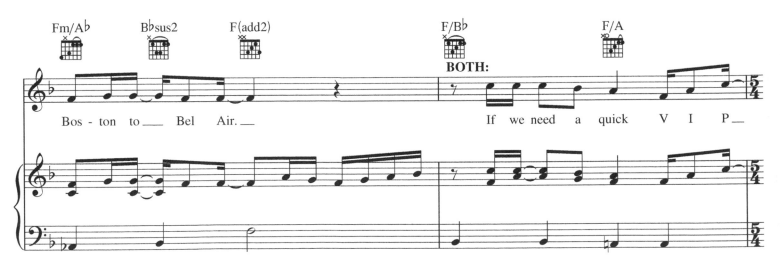

BOTH:

Bos - ton to __ Bel Air. __   If we need a quick V I P __

tick - et to *Wick-ed,* we'll get it 'cause we're pop-u - lar and part __ of it all. __

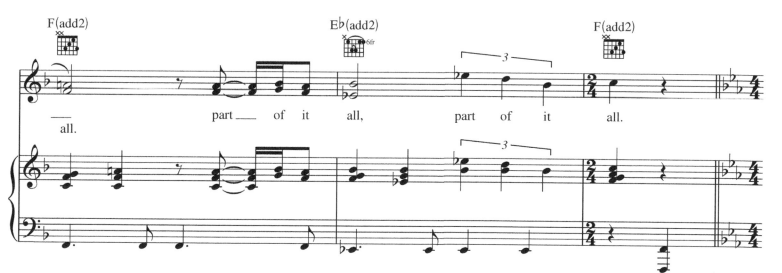

Part of it all, __
all, __ part of __ it

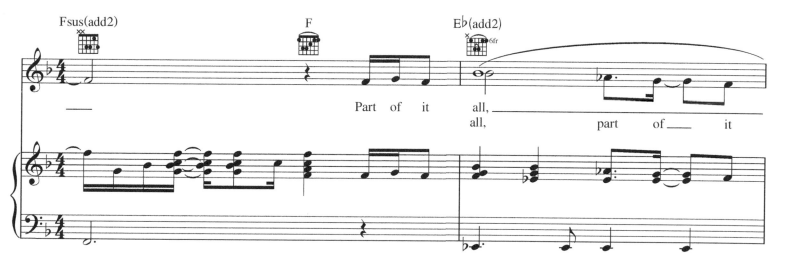

__ part __ of it all, part of it all.
all.

There'll come a day when we look back at __ the time we spent writ - ing this ver - y show.

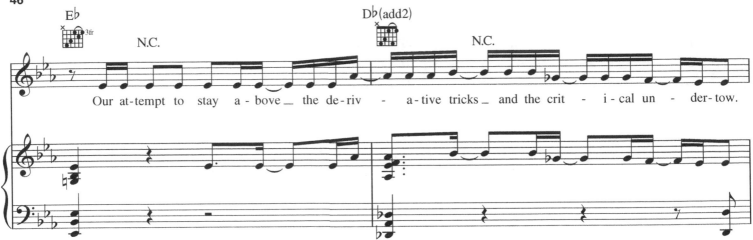

Our at-tempt to stay a-bove _ the de-riv - a-tive tricks _ and the crit - i-cal un - der-tow.

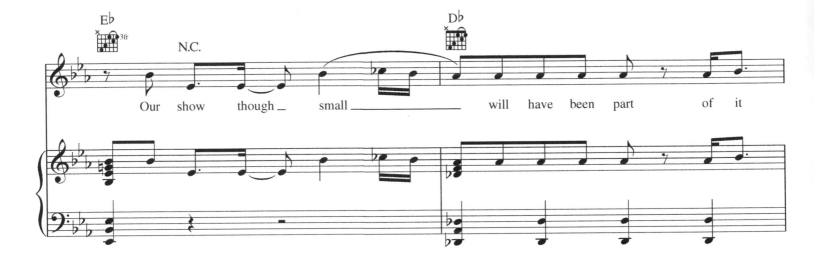

Our show though _ small ____ will have been part of it

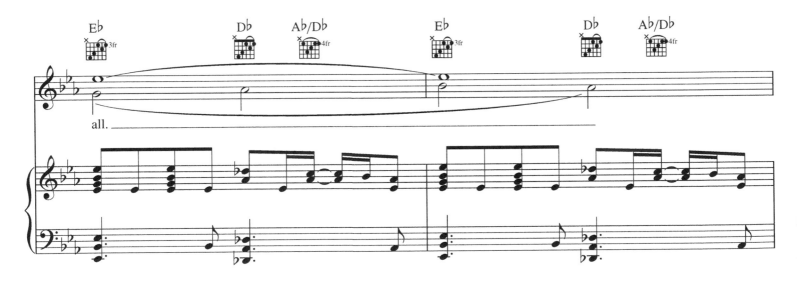

all. ____

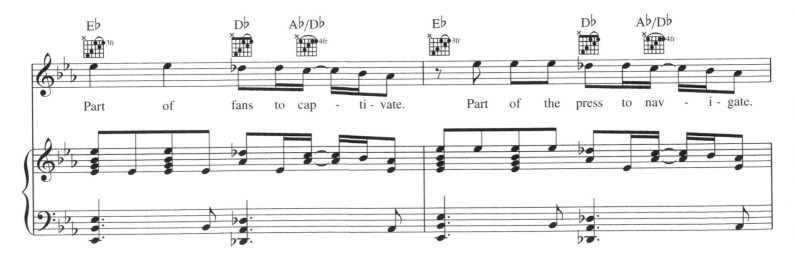

Part of fans to cap - ti-vate. Part of the press to nav - i - gate.

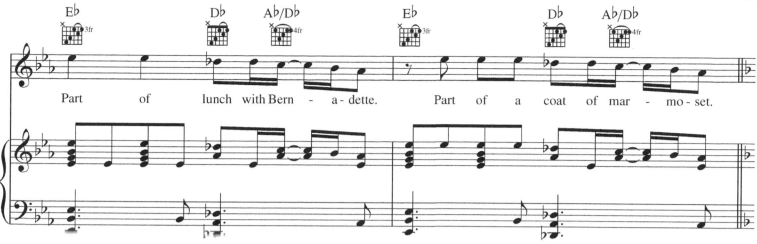

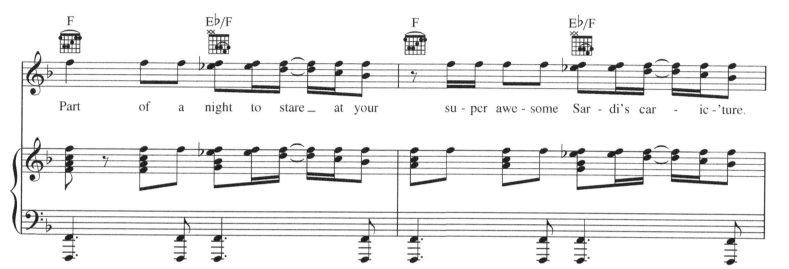

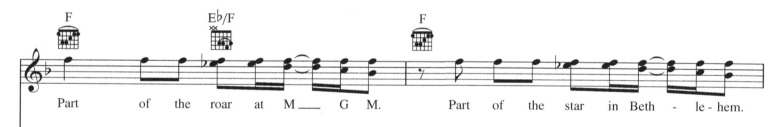

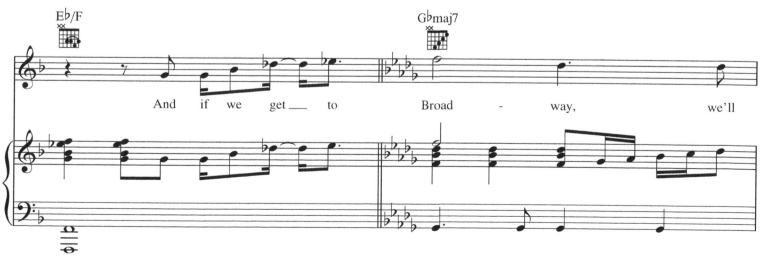

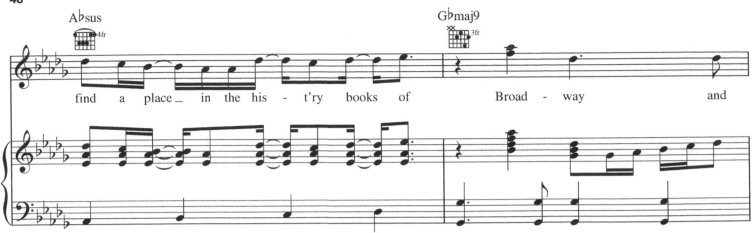

find a place___ in the his - t'ry books of Broad - way and

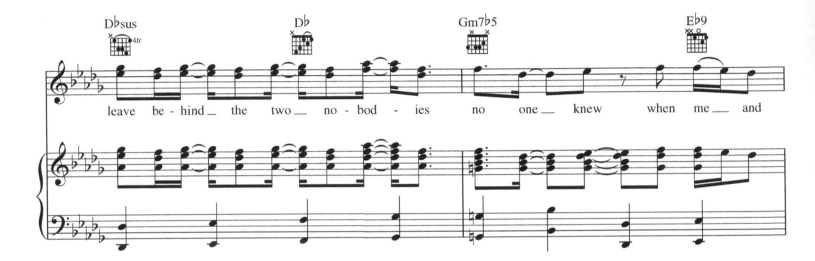

leave be - hind___ the two___ no - bod - ies no one___ knew when me___ and

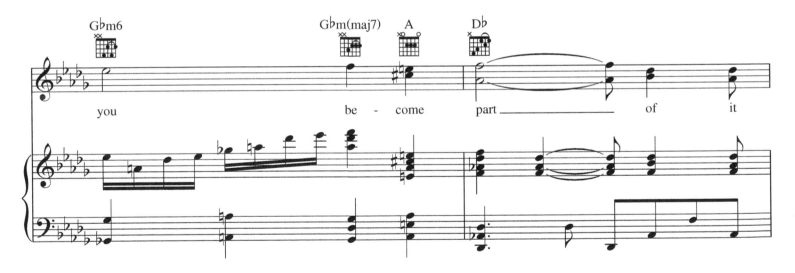

you be - come part _____ of it

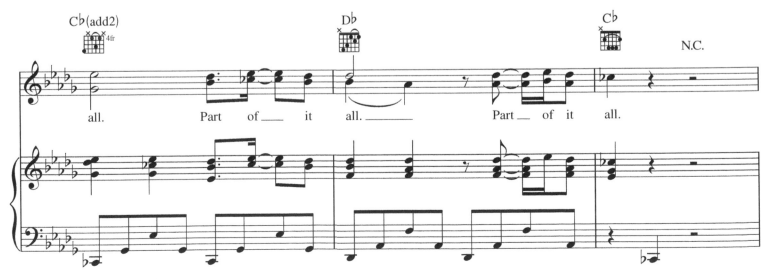

all. Part of ___ it all. _____ Part ___ of it all.

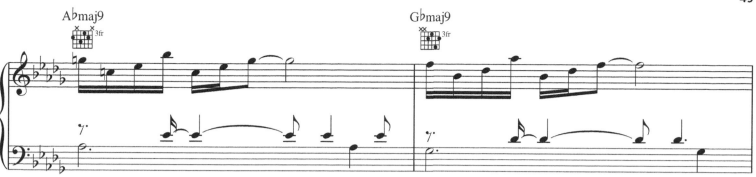

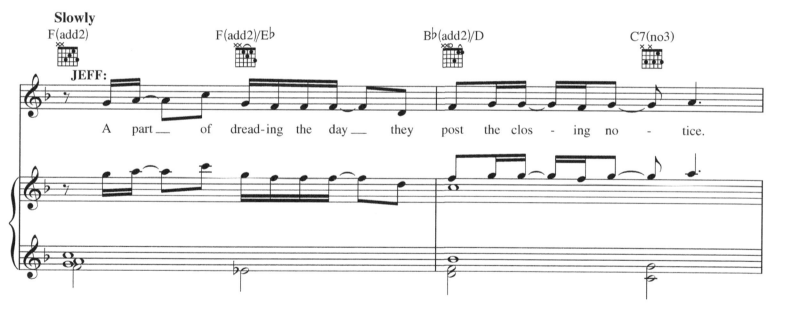

Slowly

JEFF: A part ___ of dread-ing the day ___ they post the clos - ing no - tice.

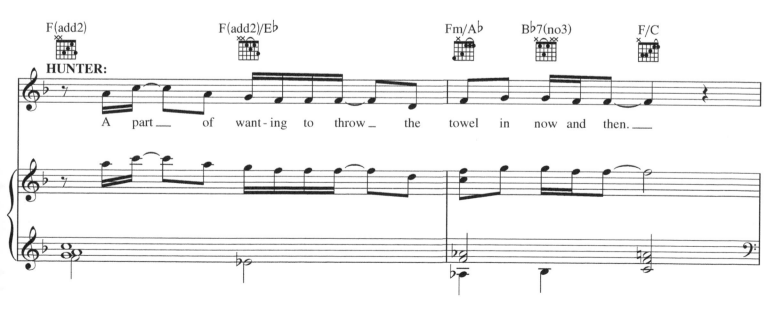

HUNTER: A part ___ of want-ing to throw ___ the towel in now and then. ___

I AM PLAYING ME

Words and Music by
JEFF BOWEN

Stuck in a show ___ where I am play-ing me. ___

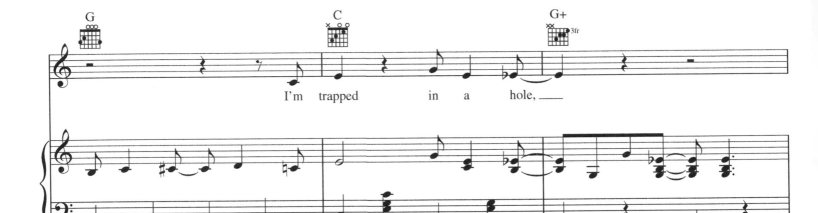

I'm trapped in a hole, ___

no - where to go with my role. Strain-in' my neck ___ for an ex -

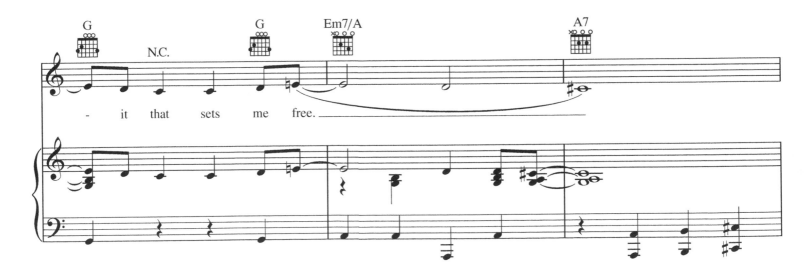

- it that sets me free. ___

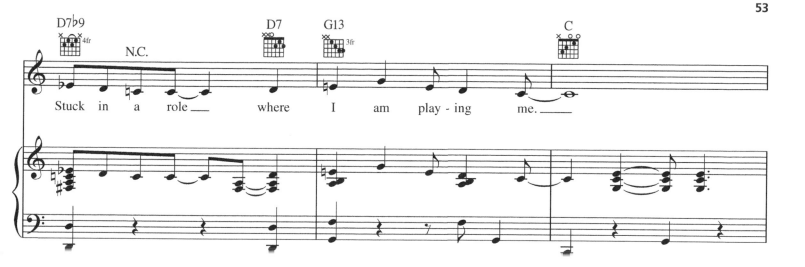

Stuck in a role ___ where I am play - ing me. ___

I in - sist I could make 'em mis - ty

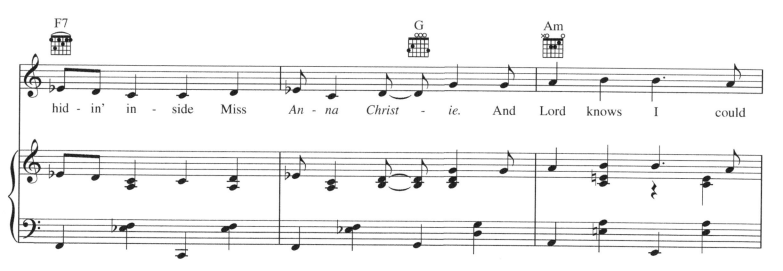

hid - in' in - side Miss *An - na Christ - ie.* And Lord knows I could

raise the roof ___ play - in' the maid ___ that goofs ___ in *Tar - tuffe.* And I could

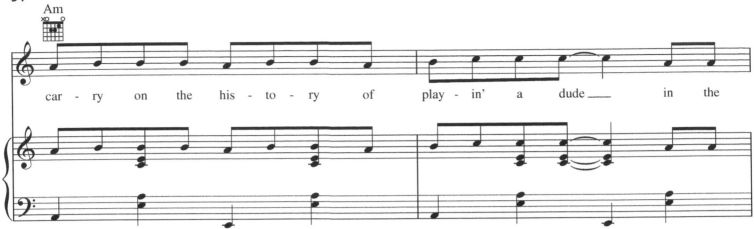

car - ry on the his - to - ry of play - in' a dude ___ in the

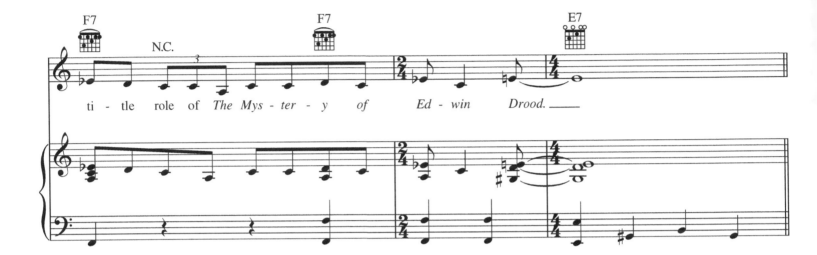

ti - tle role of *The Mys - ter - y* *of* *Ed - win* *Drood.* ___

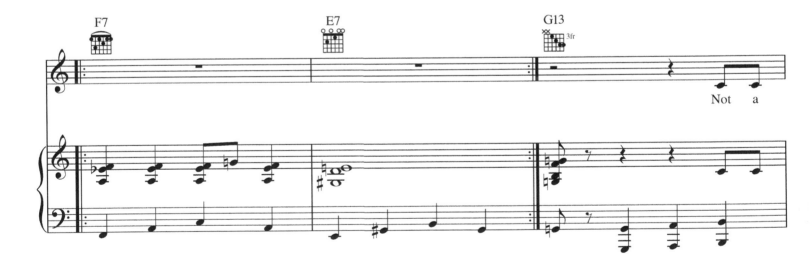

Not a

chance for my ca - reer to ad - vance ___ and there's no straight guys here for

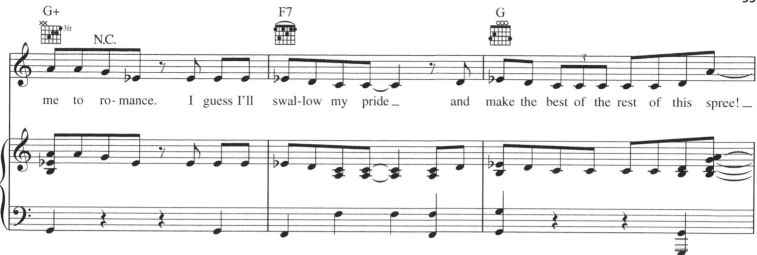

me to ro-mance. I guess I'll swal-low my pride __ and make the best of the rest of this spree! __

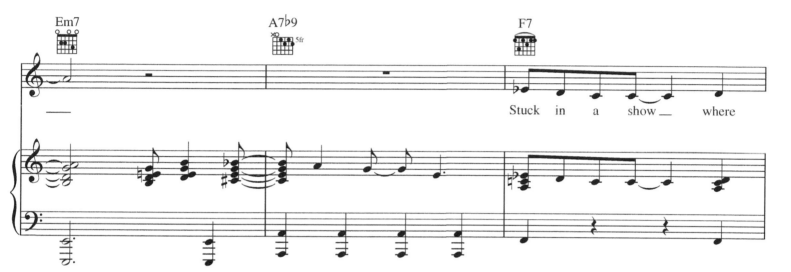

__ Stuck in a show __ where

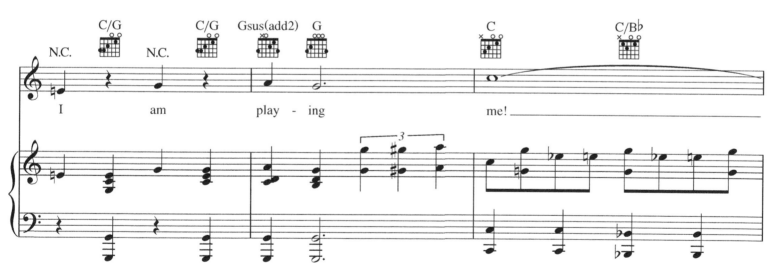

I am play - ing me! ____

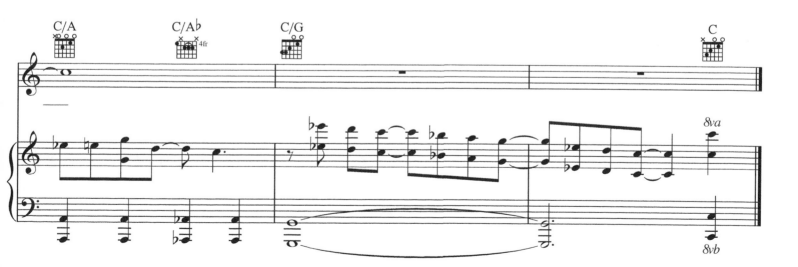

WHAT KIND OF GIRL IS SHE?

Words and Music by
JEFF BOWEN

HEIDI: I'm used to be-ing the fun-ni-est girl in the room,

that's what ev-'ry show - mo says. **SUSAN:** At least my nose could take her nose in a

cage match of nos - es. _____ **HEIDI:** *It's hard sharing the lady spotlight, Jeff.*

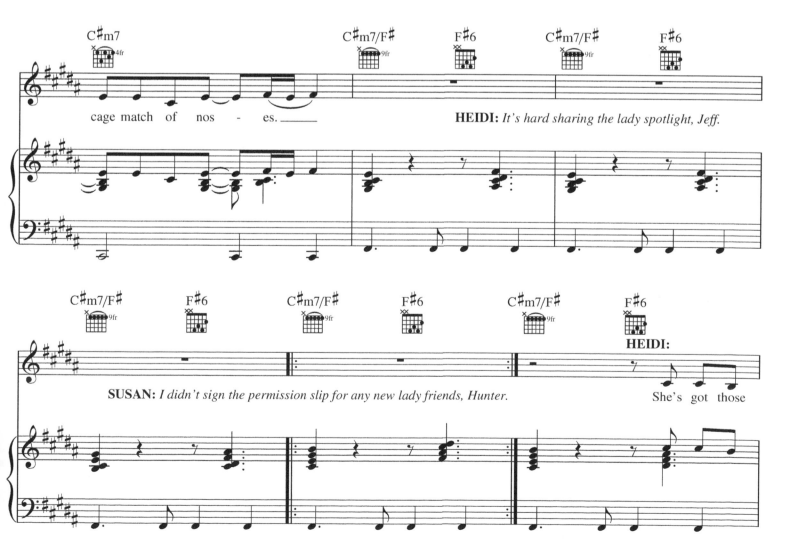

SUSAN: *I didn't sign the permission slip for any new lady friends, Hunter.*

HEIDI: She's got those

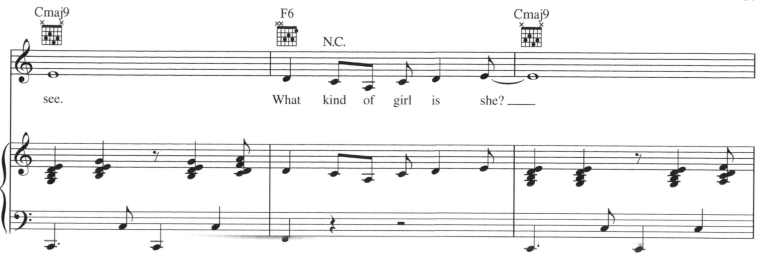

see.   What kind of girl is she? _____

What kind of girl is she? _____   What kind of girl is she? __

SUSAN:

HEIDI:

Are you gon - na eat that pick - le?

DIE VAMPIRE, DIE!

Words and Music by JEFF BOWEN
and SUSAN BLACKWELL

SUSAN: *There are some people in the world who say writing stories or composing music, or dancing sparkly dances is easy for them; nothing interferes with their ability to create. While I celebrate their creative freedom, a little part of me wants to punch those motherfuckers in the teeth. This song I sing for you guys and for all the rest of us. Help me out y'all.*

HEIDI, HUNTER & JEFF: We'll sing back-up.

SUSAN: You have a sto-ry to tell, a nov-

HEIDI, HUNTER & JEFF: -el you keep in a drawer. Old sock drawer.

SUSAN: You have a

HEIDI, HUNTER & JEFF (men at pitch):

paint-ing to paint, but you're la - zy like an old French whore. *Je____ suis____ whore.*

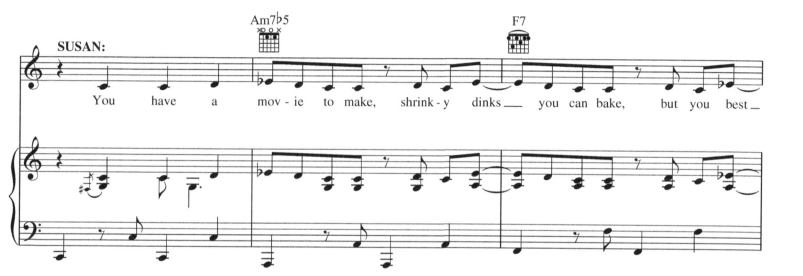

SUSAN:

You have a mov-ie to make, shrink-y dinks____ you can bake, but you best____

____ grab a stake.__ 'Cause in sweep the vam - pi - res, in_____ creep the vam - pi - res, knee____

HEIDI, HUNTER & JEFF:

Ooh _____

deep in vam-pi-res fill - ing you ___ with doubt, in-se-cu-ri-ty 'bout ___

Ooh ___

___ what your art should be, in ___ sweep the vam-pi-res. Die, ___ vam-pi - re!

Die, ___ vam-pi - re!

You sketched that tur-tle you saw in an ad ___ on late-night ca-ble T V

man - y vam - pi - res _____ in - side, out - side and

na - tion - wide. _____ It helps to

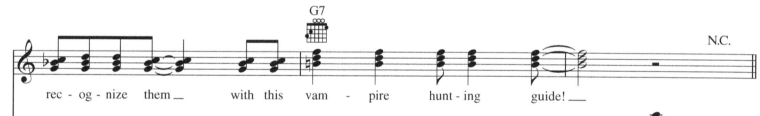

rec - og - nize them __ with this vam - pire hunt - ing guide! __

Ooh _____

SUSAN: *Listen closely, my children. A vampire is any person or thought or feeling that stands between you and your creative self-expression. They can assume many seductive forms. Here's a few of them.*

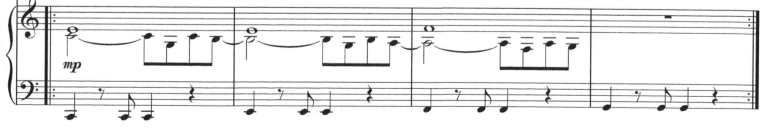

Tell us, Su - san.

SUSAN: *First up are your Pygmy Vampires. They'll swarm around you like gnats and say things like,*

HUNTER: *"Your teeth need whitening."*   **HEIDI:** *"You went to State School?"*   **JEFF:** *"You sound weird."*
HUNTER: *Shakespeare,*   **HEIDI:** *Sondheim,*   **JEFF:** *and Sedaris…*
SUSAN: *Did it before you and better than you. Or they might say you cannot sing good enough to be in a musical.*

Slower

SUSAN: **HEIDI, JEFF & HUNTER:**

Or they might say, "Your song is re - pet - i - tive. __ Your

song makes me tired. Your song is re - pet - i - tive __ and it does - n't rhyme!" __

SUSAN:

To

keep that song from you! But you tell them, "Die, Vam - pi - re, Die, ___ hie, hie!" _

HEIDI, HUNTER & JEFF:

Ooh, "Die, Vam - pi - re, Die, ___ hie, hie!" _

8vb -

Moderately, in 2

SUSAN: *Brothers and sister, next up is the Air Freshener Vampire. It might look like a Precious Moments angel with a can of Renuzit in its tiny ceramic hand.*

But don't be fooled. If it smells something unpleasant in what you're creating, it'll urge you to…
HUNTER/HEIDI/JEFF: *Pssssssst…*

SUSAN: *The last vampire is the mother of all vampires and that is the Vampire of Despair. It'll wake you up at 4 AM to say things like…*
JEFF: *Nobody cares what you think.*   **HEIDI:** *You look like an idiot.*
HUNTER: *No matter how hard you try, you'll never be good enough.*
SUSAN: *Why is it, if a stranger walked up to me on a subway platform and said these things, I'd think he was a mentally ill asshole,*
but if the vampire inside my head says it, it's the voice of reason?

Tempo I

JEFF:
You have a sto-ry to tell. ___ Pull your

nov-el out of that sock drawer.

HEIDI:
You have a

add HUNTER:
paint-ing to paint. ___ You best paint ___ it and then paint ___ some more! ___

SUSAN:
Oh, ba - by, you must es - cape, _ then grab it _ by the nape _ of the neck, _

HEIDI, HUNTER & JEFF:
Ooh _____

_ by the tra - chea. Fuck-in' break _ it, go on, _ drive the stake _ in, yeah, there's _

Ah _____

_ no mis-tak - in'. Now you're _ shak - in', bak - in'. Die, _____ vam - pire, _

Now you're _ shak - in', bak - in'.

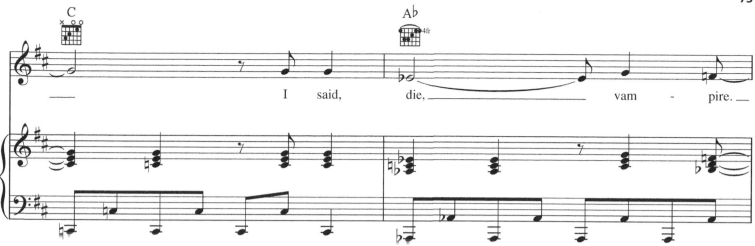

I said, die, _____ vam - pire. ___

___ I said now die vam -

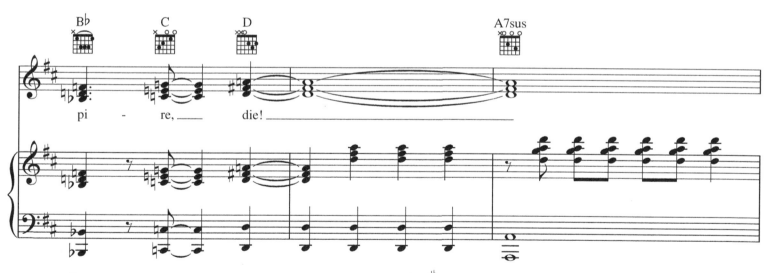

pi - re, ___ die! _____

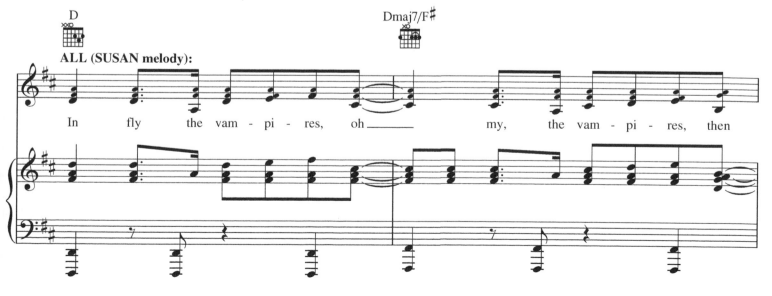

ALL (SUSAN melody):

In fly the vam - pi - res, oh _____ my, the vam - pi - res, then

SEPTEMBER SONG

Words and Music by
JEFF BOWEN

Lots of things ___ are hap-pen-in' ___ at the

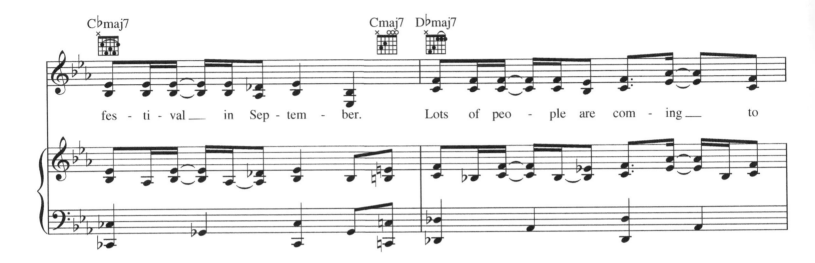

fes-ti-val ___ in Sep-tem-ber. Lots of peo-ple are com-ing ___ to

watch us do ___ our stuff. Our pants are what ___ we're crap-pin' in ___ at the

fes-ti-val ___ in Sep-tem-ber. We're nerv-ous ___ as ho-ly hell ___ and

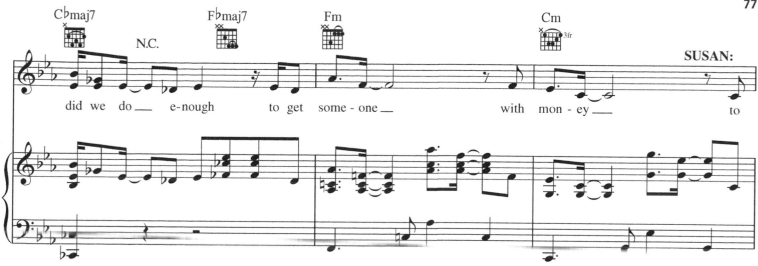

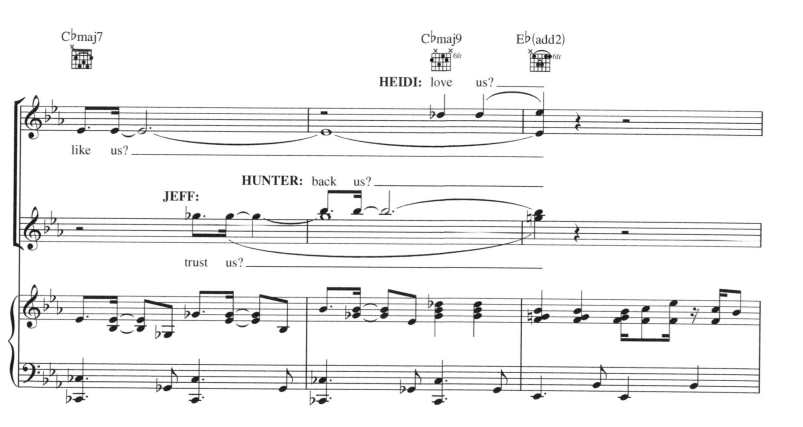

G♭maj7   A♭maj9   G♭5

JEFF & HUNTER:

veg - 'ta - ble med - ley.

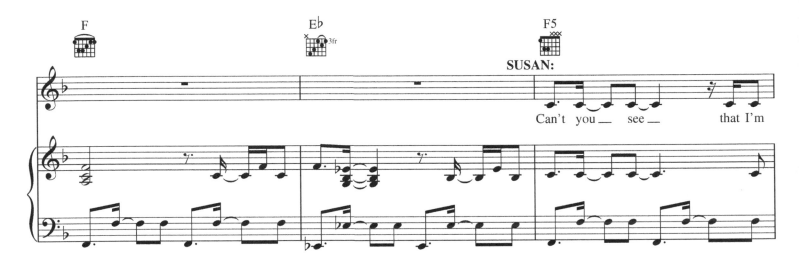

F   E♭   F5

SUSAN:

Can't you __ see __ that I'm

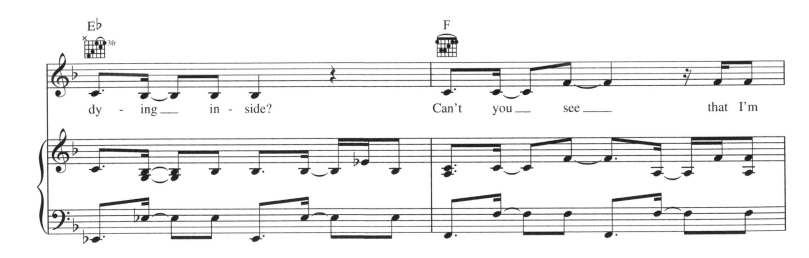

E♭   F

dy - ing __ in - side?   Can't you __ see ___ that I'm

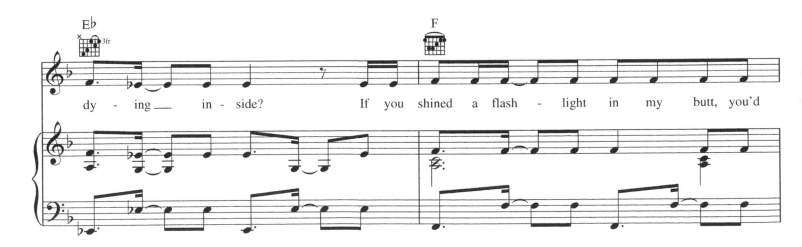

E♭   F

dy - ing __ in - side?   If you shined a flash - light in my butt, you'd

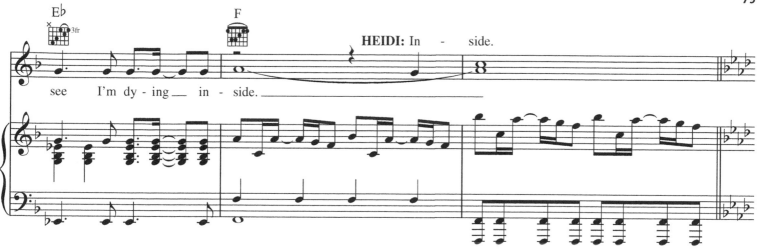

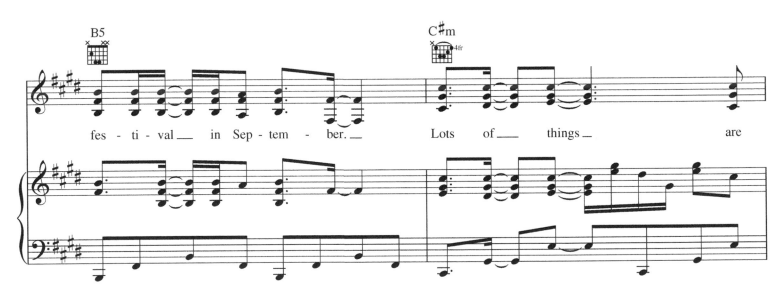

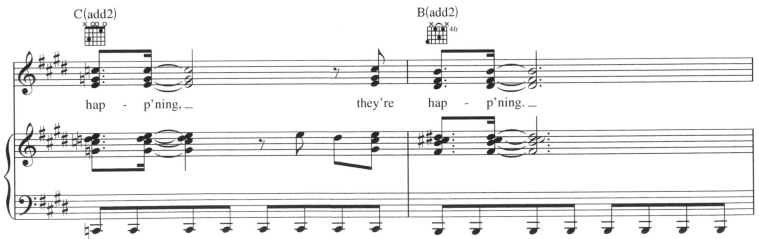

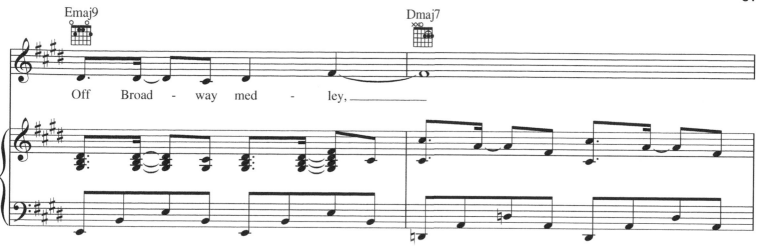

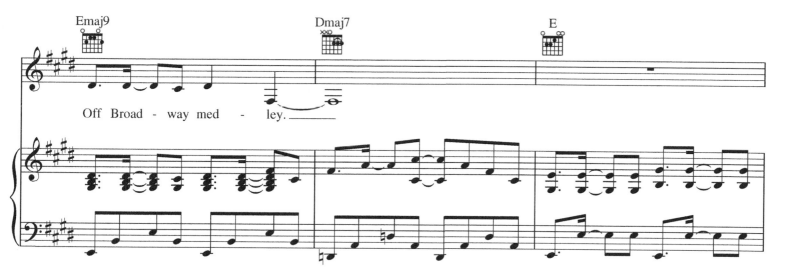

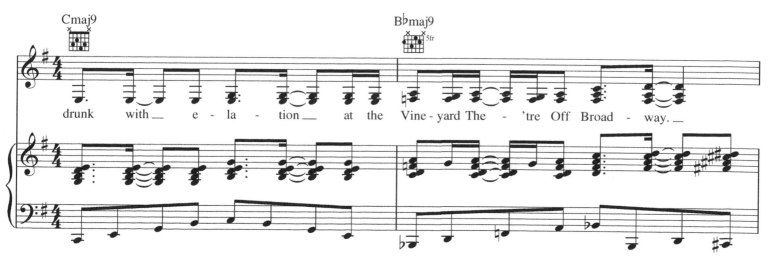

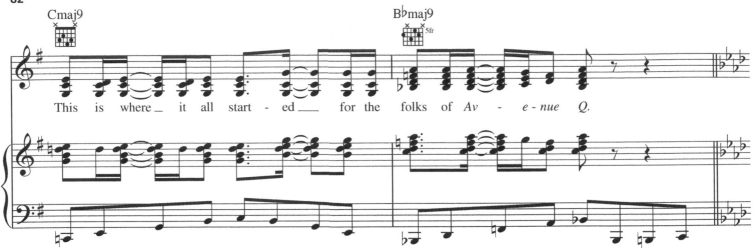

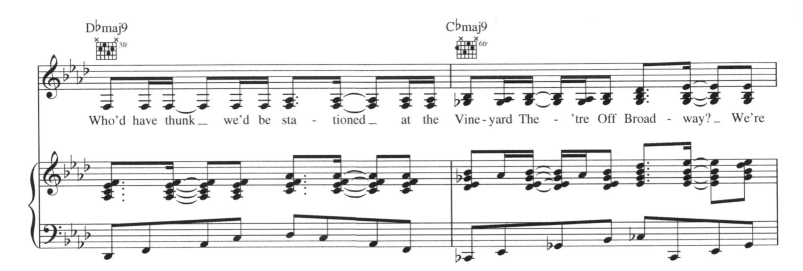

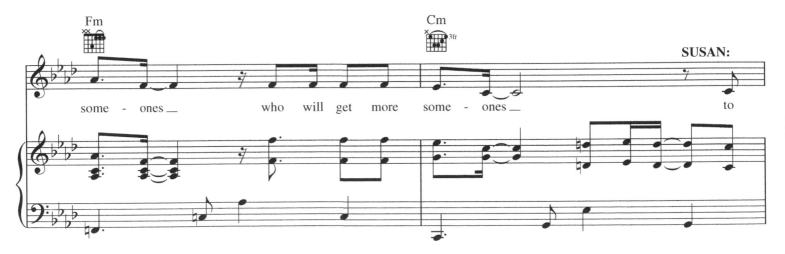

Faster

Lots of fan - cy peo - ple are

com - ing to see ___ us Off Broad - way. Ev - 'ry night ___ it seems ___ there's a

star to ___ dis - cuss! They're com - in' back - stage to meet us ___ at the

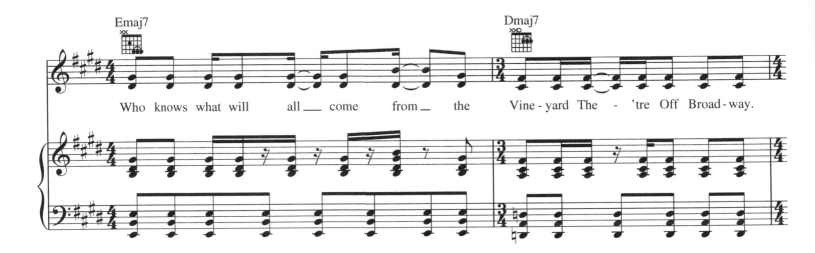

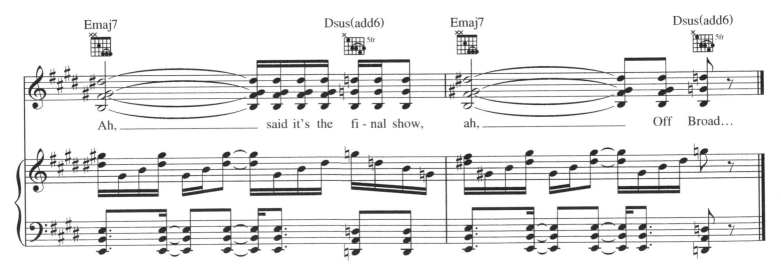

SECONDARY CHARACTERS

Words and Music by
JEFF BOWEN

Power Ballad

HEIDI: We don't have_ much time_ to dance_ in the spot - light,_ so I'm gon - na

trea - sure this Hei - di and Su - san du - et.

SUSAN: And

now may be____ the on - ly chance__ I get__ to - night__ to en - joy the

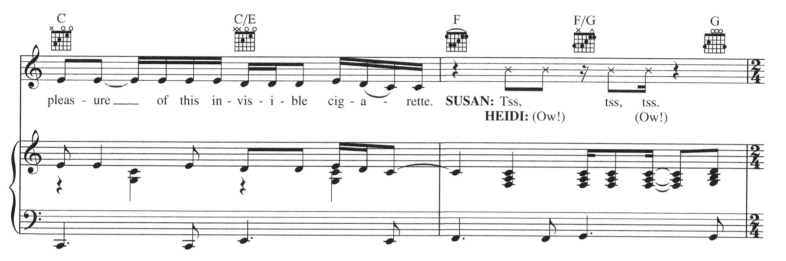

plea - sure____ of this in - vis - i - ble cig - a - rette. **SUSAN:** Tss, tss, tss.
HEIDI: (Ow!) (Ow!)

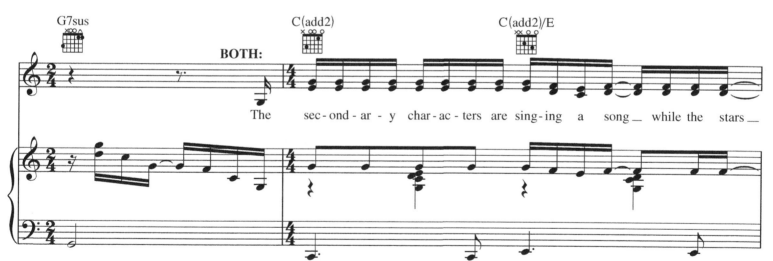

BOTH:
The sec - ond - ar - y char - ac - ters are sing - ing a song__ while the stars __

____ are snack - ing off - stage. It was their i - dea to bring__ us a - long,__ and now __

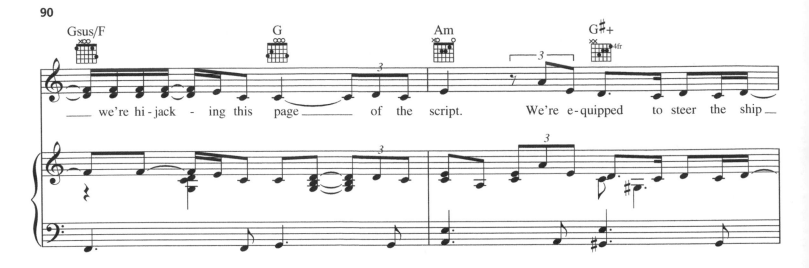

we're hi-jack-ing this page ____ of the script. We're e-quipped to steer the ship ____

____ 'til this trip-py skit ____ ends, and by the end of ____ this song we'll be best

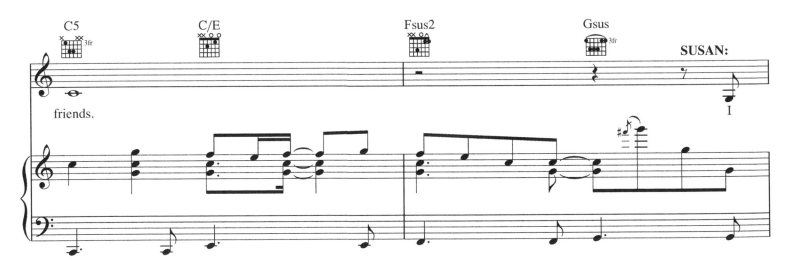

friends.

SUSAN:

I

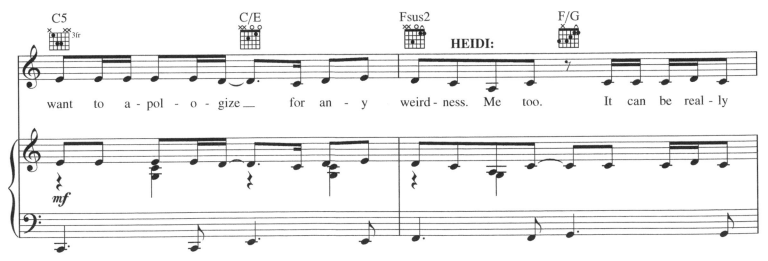

want to a-pol-o-gize ____ for an-y weird-ness. Me too. It can be real-ly

A WAY BACK TO THEN

Words and Music by
JEFF BOWEN

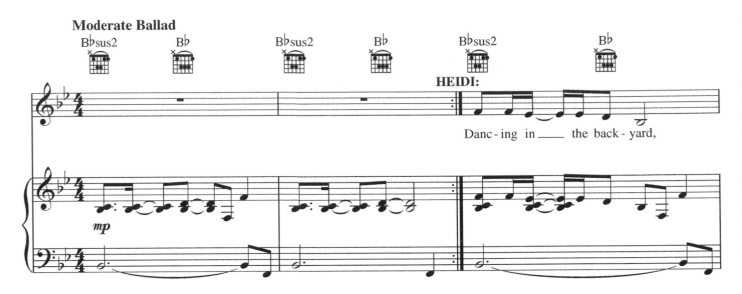

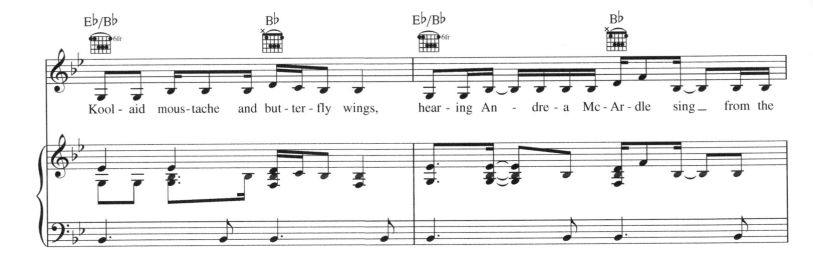

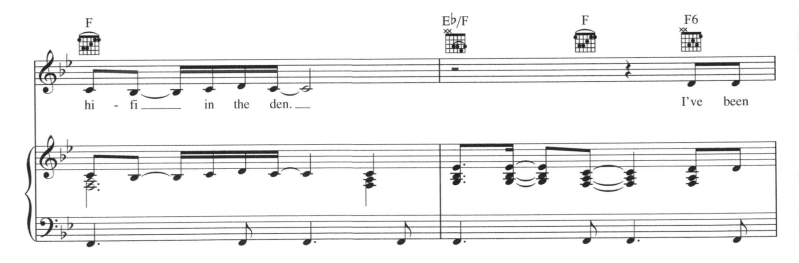

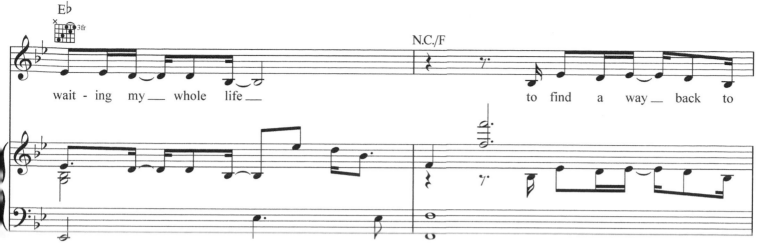

waiting my whole life to find a way back to

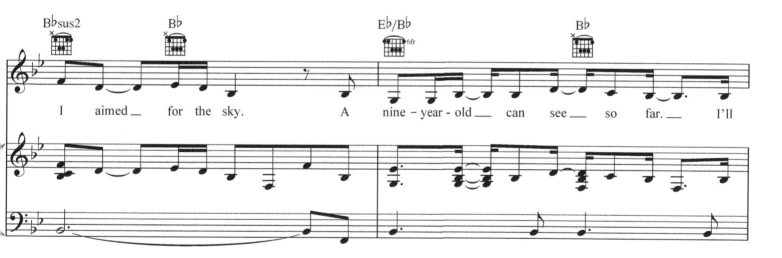

then.

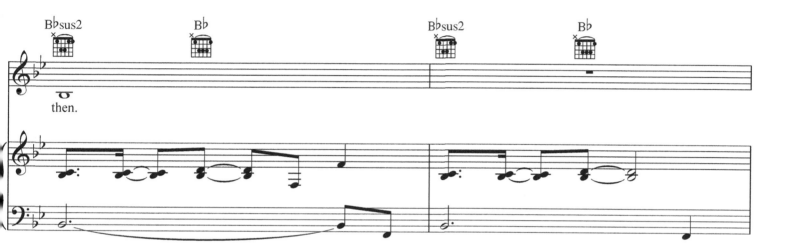

I aimed for the sky. A nine-year-old can see so far. I'll

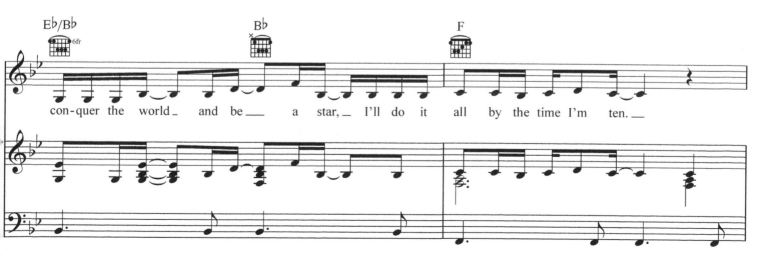

con-quer the world and be a star, I'll do it all by the time I'm ten.

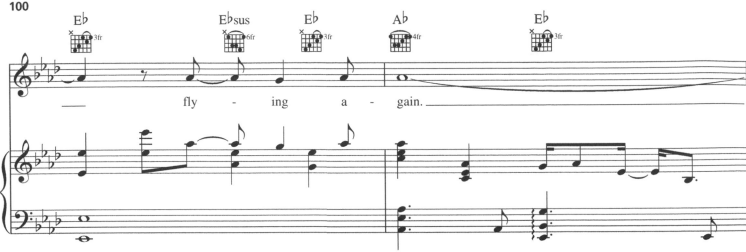

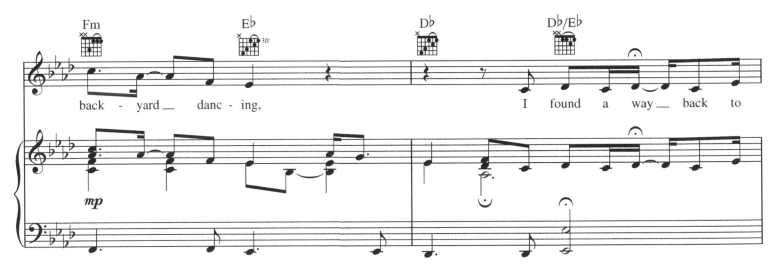

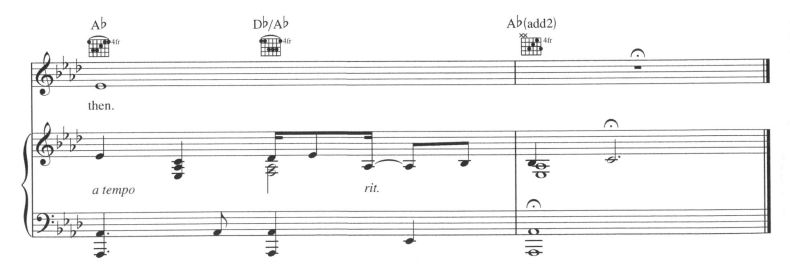

NINE PEOPLE'S FAVORITE THING

Words and Music by
JEFF BOWEN

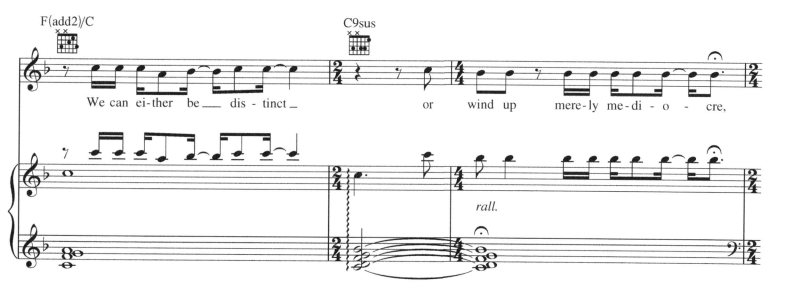

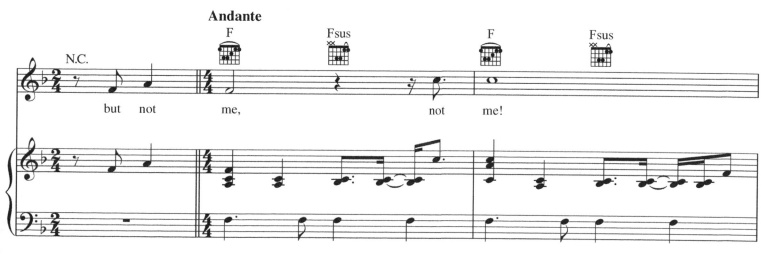

nine __ peo-ple's fa-vor-ite thing__ than a hun-dred peo-ple's ninth - fa-vor-ite

thing"?　**HUNTER:** No, you're right, Jef-fy, let's not com - pro - mise.

Let's keep mak-ing some-thing we've nev-er seen. __ A risk was tak-en with *On __ the Town,* and look what

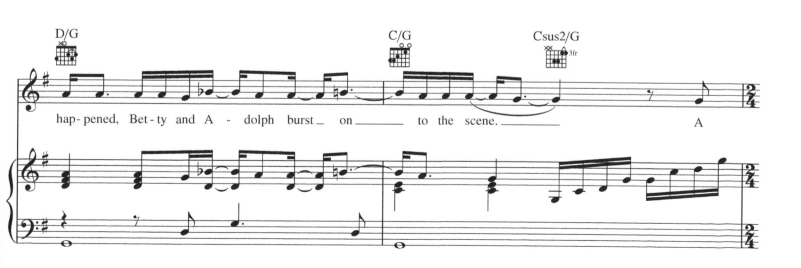

hap-pened, Bet-ty and A - dolph burst__ on_____ to the scene. _____ A

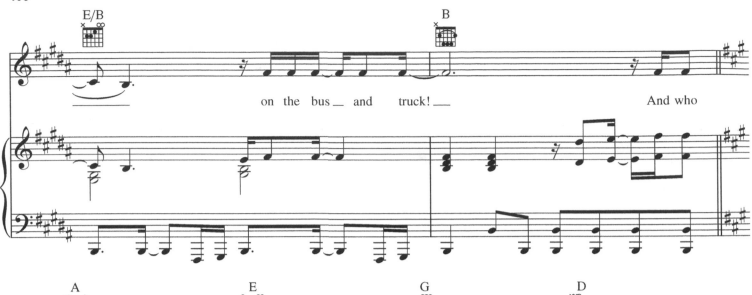

on the bus __ and truck! __ And who

says four chairs __ and a key-board __ can't __ make a Broad-way mu-si-cal? We're e-

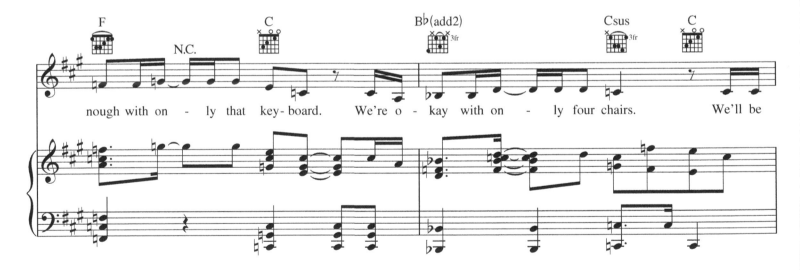

nough with on - ly that key-board. We're o - kay with on - ly four chairs. We'll be

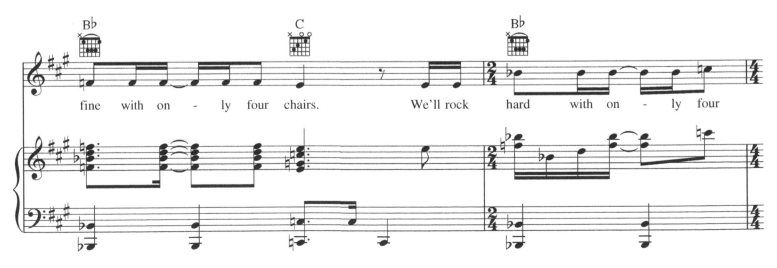

fine with on - ly four chairs. We'll rock hard with on - ly four

then we'll have eight-een peo-ple lov-in' the show. __ Then eight-een peo - ple could grow __ in - to __ five

hun - dred and twen-ty five thou - sand, six hun-dred peo - ple __ all lov - in' our

JEFF & HUNTER:

show! And may-be some day __ if we're luck-y e-nough, we'll

ALL (JEFF & HUNTER top):

all be in a stu-di-o re-cord-ing our show. __ And ten years from now __ when we play __ the cast al - bum, __